AMERICANA
A Basic Reader

AMERICANA
A Basic Reader

Pamela McPartland

Hunter College of the City University of New York

Illustrations by Alexander Kaletski

Harcourt Brace & Company

Orlando   San Diego   New York

Toronto   London   Sydney   Tokyo

ISBN: 0-15-502597-X
Library of Congress Catalog Card Number: 82-84349
Printed in the United States of America

The Woody Guthrie song lyrics quoted in chapter 10, "This Land Is Your Land," all
appear in his autobiography, *Bound for Glory* (New York: E. P. Dutton & Co., Inc.,
1976). The lines from "Bling-Blang," words and music by Woody Guthrie, are copyright © 1954 and renewed 1982 by Folkways Music Publishers, Inc., New York,
N.Y., and are used by permission; the lines from "This Land Is Your Land," words
and music by Woody Guthrie, are copyright © 1956, 1958 and 1970 by Ludlow
Music, Inc., New York, N.Y., and are used by permission; the lines from "I Didn't
Boil Myself No Coffee, etc.," words and music by Woody Guthrie, are copyright ©
1943 and revised 1971 by Marjorie Guthrie, New York, N.Y., and are also used by
permission.

Picture credits:
Cover and chapter opening art by Alexander Kaletski.
p. 20: Courtesy of Standard Oil; p. 26: New York Convention and Visitors Bureau;
p. 44: National Archives; p. 49: National Archives; p. 60: UPI; p. 61: Standard Oil
of New Jersey.

For Ryan, Sean, and James

To the Instructor

Americana is a reading text for elementary to intermediate level students of English as a second language. The reading material is geared to young adults and adults learning English in the United States or abroad. As the title indicates, the book is a collection of stories about America—its people and its history.

Before having the students read the stories, use the chapter opening illustration and the title as the basis for a pre-reading discussion. This will help the students focus on the topic and obtain some information about the topic before reading. This is also a good opportunity for the students to work in groups. Each student can tell the group what he or she thinks the passage is about. Then the group can discuss what they already know about the subject. Each group might give a report to the class.

Next, the students should read the story silently. (There will be other activities for reading out loud, later in the chapter.) If possible, the chapters should be covered in sequence, because the stories get longer and students will be able to see their progress as they work through the book.

Each story is followed by several exercises. By doing the exercises, students will learn to:
- answer true/false comprehension questions.
- write the answers to comprehension questions.
- make inferences.
- identify the appropriate meaning when a word has more than one meaning.
- use new vocabulary words.
- identify word forms (nouns, verbs, adjectives) in context.
- become aware of function words (prepositions) and how they are used in English.
- reduce stress on the function words when reading aloud.
- spell numbers.
- put words together to form complete sentences.
- do some creative writing and improvisation.
- identify "chunks" of meaning.
- process larger bits of information by reading in "chunks."
- place the stress on the correct syllable in new vocabulary words.

In later chapters, students will also learn to:

- scan a page for specific information.
- use synonyms and antonyms.

Because *Americana* is designed for beginners, there is redundancy throughout the text. In each chapter, the story is repeated for the "Prepositions" exercise and for the "Chunking" exercise.

Americana contains ten chapters. Students should be able to finish the book in one course. This gives elementary-level students a sense of accomplishment.

Unlike other low-level reading texts, *Americana* contains exercises to help students recognize that a sentence consists of meaningful "chunks" of words (for example, the complete subject, verb, object/complement, adverbial). Many students learning a second language view a sentence as a string of individual words. The "Chunking" exercises will help students identify the words that form one "chunk" of meaning. Such exercises will make students active readers and will help them learn to capture the natural phrasing of a sentence. Students can identify small chunks initially, but should be encouraged to process larger chunks as they get more practice. If students have trouble grasping the concept of chunking, read the story out loud, pausing after each thought group, while the students follow in their books and put a slash mark at each pause. By doing other exercises, like "Make a Sentence" (also based on chunking), students will gradually grasp the idea of processing groups of words, rather than individual words.

Although numbers may not seem particularly relevant to a reading textbook, I have included short exercises on spelling out numbers in each chapter because of the importance of numbers in everyday life.

Of course, it is not necessary to have the students do all the exercises. Select the exercises that meet the needs of your particular group of students and do only those exercises. The important thing is that the students enjoy reading in their new language. *Americana* was written to provide students who are just starting to learn English with stories about a topic they are interested in—America.

My first thank-you goes to Peter Vajda, of New York University's American Language Institute, for giving me, way back when, some tips on teaching reading to beginners. A formal thank-you goes to Professors Arthur Bronstein, D. Terence Langendoen, Robert Vago, and Miroslav Rensky, of the CUNY Graduate School and University Center, for their professional insights into the English language. A secret thank-you goes to Frank Smith, whom I've never met, but whose work on teaching reading greatly influenced the approach taken in this book. A warm thank-you goes to my colleagues at the Hunter College International English Language Institute, Betsy Reitbauer and Eric Grumbacher, for field-testing the material and making suggestions for improvement. A word of thanks and congratulations goes to Victoria Henriquez, an ESL student at the Institute, who typed the manuscript. And a very special thank-you to Albert Richards, Cecilia Gardner, Nancy Kirsh, Harriet Meltzer, and Geri Davis of Harcourt Brace Jovanovich for the enthusiasm with which they worked on this project.

Most of all, I'd like to thank Alexander Kaletski, my illustrator, sample student, editor, and disciplinarian, without whose help this book would still be just an idea.

Pamela McPartland

To the Student

Americana is a reader for students of English as a second language. As the title indicates, the book is a collection of stories about America*—its people and its history.

Each story in the book is longer than the previous story. The first story has 122 words. The last story has 361 words.

By doing the exercises in the book you will learn to:

- answer questions about the stories.
- make inferences. (An inference is something the story doesn't tell you directly. You can guess it from the story.)
- figure out the meanings of words from the sentences they are in.
- guess the correct meaning when a word has more than one meaning.
- read in groups of words, instead of word by word.
- use new words in writing and in conversation.

* "America" is used in this book to mean the United States only.

Contents

1

2

3

The Stars and Stripes   31

4

Uncle Sam   41

✒ 5 ✒

1600 Pennsylvania Avenue, Washington, D.C. 53

✒ 6 ✒

The First Oil Well in the World   65

7

8

9

Fall Back, Spring Ahead — 105

10

This Land Is Your Land — 117

Before reading each story,

- look at the picture.

- read the title of the story.

- say what you think the story is about.

- discuss what you already know about the topic.

As you read the story,

- relax.

- don't try to remember everything.

- don't think about the pronunciation of the words.

- don't translate into your native language.

- don't stop when you see a new word—just keep reading.

- look for the general idea of the story.

The most important thing is to enjoy the stories.

1

The Discovery of America

Christopher Columbus was born in Genoa, Italy. He loved the sea. When he was only fourteen, he became a sailor. Later, he became an explorer. He wanted to discover a new route to India. The Spanish queen, Isabella, gave him three ships, sailors, and money for his trip.

Columbus and his sailors were at sea for ten weeks. Finally, on October 12, 1492, they saw land. Columbus thought it was India. He called the people there "Indians." Columbus didn't discover a new route to India; he discovered a new land.

Later, Amerigo Vespucci, another Italian explorer, wrote about this new land. A German mapmaker* read Amerigo's stories. He liked them so much that on the map of Columbus's India, he wrote "America"!

122 words

---

* Martin Waldseemuller. His map was printed in 1507.

3

Comprehension Questions

A. Answer true or false.

Example: Columbus was born in Italy. _____*True*_____

1. Columbus wanted to discover a new route to India. _____

2. The Italian queen gave Columbus ships, sailors, and money. _____

3. Columbus was at sea for ten weeks. _____

4. Columbus saw land on October 12, 1492. _____

5. Columbus knew it was a new land. _____

6. Columbus called the people on the land "Italians." _____

7. Columbus discovered a new land. _____

8. Amerigo Vespucci was another Italian explorer. _____

9. Amerigo Vespucci called the new land "America." _____

B. Write the answer "Yes, he did" or "No, he didn't."

Example: Did Columbus become an explorer?

   Yes, he did. _____

1. Did the Spanish king help Columbus?

   _____

2. Did Columbus discover America?

   _____

3. Did Columbus call the people there "Indians"?

   _____

4. Did Columbus see India?

_____

5. Did Amerigo Vespucci write about this new land?

_____

Inference Questions

Answer true or false.

1. America was not on the map before Columbus's trip. _____

2. A German mapmaker gave America its name. _____

3. Nobody lived in America before 1492. _____

Words with More Than One Meaning

Mark the answer that gives the correct meaning of the underlined word in each sentence.

Example: The Spanish queen, Isabella, gave him three ships, sailors, and money for his trip.

  (X)a. voyage, journey (noun)
  ( )b. to almost fall down (verb)

1. Finally, on October 12, 1492, they saw land.

  ( )a. an instrument to cut wood (noun)
  ( )b. looked at, viewed (verb)

2. He called the people there "Indians."

  ( )a. telephoned (verb)
  ( )b. named (verb)

3. Columbus didn't discover a new route to India; he discovered a new land.

    ( )a. to bring (a plane) down (verb)
    ( )b. a country (noun)

Vocabulary Practice

A. Fill in each blank with the correct word.

Example: An explorer wants to _____*discover*_____ a new land.

map	sea	discover	read
queen	born	October	trip
route	became	discovery	
later	called	German	

1. The bus took a different _____ today.

2. She is a good swimmer because she lives near the _____.

3. If he makes a lot of money, he will take a _____ around the world.

4. If you get lost on the subway, look at the subway _____.

5. We just _____ a story about the discovery of America.

6. She was _____ in Italy, but she lived in Spain.

7. He was a good sailor, so he _____ a captain very fast.

8. Bonn is a _____ city.

9. I don't want to do it now. I'll do it _____.

10. His name was James, but everybody _____ him Jim.

11. _____ is the tenth month of the year.

12. Cleopatra was an Egyptian _____.

13. Penicillin was an important medical _____.

B. Fill in each blank with the correct word. Then read the dialogue to the class.

October	sea	became	thought	sailor
ship	singer	stories	land	money

A. Where's your son these days?

B. He's at _____ right now.

A. Is he a _____?

B. He wanted to be a _____, but it isn't easy for a

singer to make _____. He didn't have a regular job,

so he joined the navy and _____ a sailor.

A. I _____ he was only sixteen.

B. No, he turned seventeen in _____.

A. I bet he'll have a lot of _____ to tell when he comes home.

B. I don't think so. What can happen on a _____?

A. Not on the ship, on the _____!

Word Forms
A. Choose the correct word form for each sentence.

1. *Italy   Italian*

   a. Rome is the capital of _____.

   b. Pizza is an _____ dish.

2. *Spain   Spanish*

    a. "Gato" is the _____ word for "cat."

    b. Seville is a city in _____.

3. *Germany   German*

    a. Munich is a city in _____.

    b. Beck's is a _____ beer.

4. *India   Indian*

    a. _____ is in southern Asia.

    b. The Cherokee and Choctaw are _____ tribes.

5. *America   American*

    a. Ernest Hemingway is a great _____ writer.

    b. The United States is in North _____.

Can you write your own sentences?

6. *France   French*

    a. _____

    b. _____

7. *Japan   Japanese*

    a. _____

    b. _____

8. *Poland   Polish*

    a. _____

    b. _____

B. Choose the correct word form for each sentence.

1. *sail   sailor*

   a. He became a _____.

   b. He wanted to _____ across the Atlantic Ocean.

2. *explore   explorer*

   a. Amerigo Vespucci was an Italian _____.

   b. He wanted to _____ the New World.

3. *discover   discovery*

   a. Columbus wanted to _____ a new route to India.

   b. His _____ was a surprise.

4. *write   writer*

   a. Mark Twain was an American _____.

   b. Please _____ your name and address here.

5. *read   reader*

   a. She is a fast _____.

   b. She loves to _____.

Prepositions

A. Write the correct preposition in each blank.

about   for   in   on   to

Christopher Columbus was born _____ Genoa, Italy. He loved the sea. When he was only fourteen, he became a sailor. Later, he became an

explorer. He wanted to discover a new route _____ India. The Span-
                                                2

ish queen, Isabella, gave him three ships, sailors, and money _____
                                                                  3

his trip.

Columbus and his sailors were at sea _____ ten weeks. Finally,
                                          4

_____ October 12, 1492, they saw land. Columbus thought it was
    5

India. He called the people there "Indians." Columbus didn't discover a new

route _____ India; he discovered a new land.
          6

Later, Amerigo Vespucci, another Italian explorer, wrote _____
                                                              7

this new land. A German mapmaker read Amerigo's stories. He liked them

so much that _____ the map of Columbus's India, he wrote "Amer-
                  8

ica"!

B. In English, one-syllable prepositions are spoken very softly (without stress). Read the story out loud, whispering the prepositions: *for, in, on, to.* (*About* is a two-syllable preposition.)

Numbers

A. Write the words for the numbers. (These numbers are in the story.)

1. 3 _____

2. 10 _____

3. 14 _____

B. Write the numbers for the words. (These numbers are in the story.)

1. twelve _____

2. fourteen ninety-two _____

Make a Sentence

Choose one subject, one verb, and one object to make a complete sentence. Draw lines to connect the parts of your sentences. Make three sentences from each of the three groups of sentence parts given here. One sentence has been made for you in the first group.

Subject	*Verb*	*Object/Complement*
1. Christopher Columbus	gave	land.
2. The Spanish queen	saw	the sea.
3. The sailors	loved	him three ships.
4. Columbus	didn't discover	the people "Indians."
5. He	called	a new land.
6. Columbus	discovered	a new route to India.
7. Amerigo Vespucci	liked	this new land.
8. A German mapmaker	read	them.
9. He	wrote about	Amerigo's stories.

Creative Writing

Write a story about *your* discovery of a new land or planet. Fill in each blank with a word that fits into your story.

THE DISCOVERY OF _____
                        1

I was born in _____. I loved
                  2

_____. When I was only _____, I
        3   4

became a/an _____. Later, I became a/an
                  5

_____. I wanted to discover _____.
        6   7

_____ gave me _____ for my trip.
        8   9

I was _____ for ten _____. Fi-
            10   11

nally, on _____, I saw _____. I
                12   13

thought it was _____. I called the people there
                          14

_____. I didn't discover _____; I
          15   16

discovered a new _____.
                          17

Dialogue and Improvisation

Fill in the missing parts of the dialogue. Work with a partner. Read the
dialogue to the class.

A.
   —Are you going to the parade today?
   —What parade?
   —The Columbus Day Parade!
   —Who's Columbus?
   —Columbus was _____.
   —What did he do?
   —He _____.
   —When?
   —On _____.
   —Oh! _____.

B.
   —Why is America called "America"?
   —It was named after Amerigo Vespucci.
   —Did he discover America?
   —No, _____.
   —Then why wasn't it called "Christopherica"?
   —Because a mapmaker read _____ and
   wrote _____ on the map of Columbus's
   India.
   —That's too bad for Christopher Columbus!
   —Not really. We have a Columbus Day, but we don't have a Vespucci
   Day.
   —Yes, _____.

Chunking

When you read in your native language, you don't read one word at a time.
Instead, you read words in meaningful groups, or chunks. In the next
exercise, you will learn to read in chunks, in English. When you chunk

words, it is easier to understand the meaning of the sentence. But it is necessary to group the words correctly.

For example, if you read this sentence word by word, without chunking, it is difficult to understand:

After   /   class,   /   I'm   /   going   /   to   /   the   /   movies.

If you chunk the words incorrectly, it is also difficult to understand the sentences:

After   /   class I'm   /   going to the   /   movies.

But if you chunk the words correctly, it is easy to understand the sentence:

After class,   /   I'm going   /   to the movies.
  (When?)   (What?)   (Where?)

Each of these chunks carries some of the meaning of the sentence. "After class" tells you *when* the action of the sentence will take place, "I'm going" tells you *what* will happen, and "to the movies" tells you *where*.

If you *speak* in chunks, it is also easier for people to understand you.

The following rules will help you divide your sentences into chunks:

Rules for Chunking	*Example*
1. the complete subject	Christopher Columbus
2. the complete verb	was born
3. the complete phrase	in Genoa, Italy
4. the complete object or complement	an explorer
5. a one-word subject + a one-word verb	he called
or	
a one-word verb + a one-word object	wrote "America"!
6. a complete clause	When he was only fourteen,
7. the words between commas	. . ., Amerigo Vespucci, . . .
8. words between a period and a comma	.Later, . . .
9. a short simple sentence	He loved the sea.

A. Under each chunk in the story below, write the number of the rule the chunk follows. For example:

/   <u>Christopher Columbus</u>   /
1 (the complete subject)

/   <u>was born</u>   /
2 (the complete verb)

B. Read the story silently. Read in chunks, not word by word.

C. Read the story out loud to the class. Remember, read in chunks. Stop only where you see a line like this: /

Christopher Columbus   /   was born   /   in Genoa, Italy.   /   He loved
<u>1</u>   <u>2</u>

the sea.   /   When he was only fourteen,   /   he became   /   a sailor.   /

Later,   /   he became   /   an explorer.   /   He wanted to discover   /

a new route to India.   /   The Spanish queen,   /   Isabella,   /   gave

him   /   three ships,   /   sailors,   /   and money   /   for his trip.   /

Columbus and his sailors   /   were at sea   /   for ten weeks.   /   Fi-

nally,   /   on October 12,   /   1492,   /   they saw land.   /   Columbus

thought   /   it was India.   /   He called   /   the people there "Indians."   /

Columbus didn't discover   /   a new route to India;   /   he discovered   /

a new land.   /

Later,   /   Amerigo Vespucci,   /   another Italian explorer,   /   wrote

about   /   this new land.   /   A German mapmaker   /   read Amerigo's

stories.   /   He liked them so much that   /   on the map of Columbus's

India,   /   he wrote "America"!   /

Vocabulary List

The following words are listed as they appear in the story. The dictionary form is given in parentheses. Read the words out loud. Pay attention to the stress and the number of syllables in each word.

Adjectives	*Nouns*	*Verbs*	*Adverbs*
new	dis·cóv·er·y	was born (bear)	lát·er
an·óth·er	A·mér·i·ca	loved (love)	there
Spán·ish	sea	be·cáme (become)	
three	fóur·téen	wánt·ed (want)	
ten	sáil·or	dis·cóv·er	
Gér·man	ex·plór·er	gave (give)	
	route	saw (see)	
	Ín·di·a	thought (think)	
	queen	called (call)	
	ships (ship)	wrote (write)	
	món·ey	wrote a·bóut (write)	
	trip	read (read)	
	weeks (week)	liked (like)	
	Oc·tó·ber		
	land		
	péo·ple (person)		
	Ín·di·ans (Indian)		
	map		
	mápmak·er		
	stó·ries (story)		

2

Ms. Liberty

She lives alone on an island, but she isn't lonely. She has visitors all the time. They come to admire her beauty and her size. She is very tall—ninety-two meters. In her right hand, she holds a torch. In her left hand, she holds a tablet with the date July 4, 1776.* She wears a copper crown.

She came to America from France in 1885. She arrived in New York in many boxes. It was a big job to put her together. It took one year.

She stands on a pedestal made in America. On the base of the pedestal, it says, " . . . I lift my lamp beside the golden door." She welcomes immigrants and visitors to this land.

She is a national monument and a symbol of freedom. She is the Statue of Liberty. Her full name is "Liberty Enlightening the World."

> 143 words

* On this date the American colonies declared their independence from England. July 4 is a national holiday, called Independence Day.

Comprehension Questions

A. Answer true or false.

Example: Many people go to see the Statue of Liberty. _____*True*_____

1. The Statue of Liberty is very tall and beautiful. _____

2. The statue has a torch in its left hand. _____

3. The statue has a tablet in its right hand. _____

4. The date on the tablet is July 4, 1976. _____

5. The statue was made in France. _____

6. The pedestal was also made in France. _____

B. Write the answer "Yes, it is" or "No, it isn't."

Example: Is the Statue of Liberty on an island?

　　　　Yes, it is. _____

1. Is the statue ninety-two meters tall?

　　_____

2. Is the crown gold?

　　_____

3. Is the statue a national monument?

　　_____

Inference Questions

Answer true or false.

1. The Statue of Liberty is in France. _____

2. The Statue of Liberty is a popular monument. _____

3. The Statue of Liberty is a statue of a woman. _____

4. The Statue of Liberty is always called "Liberty Enlightening the World."

Words with More Than One Meaning

Mark the answer that gives the correct meaning of the underlined word in each sentence.

1. In her right hand, she holds a torch.

    ( )a. opposite of left (adjective)
    ( )b. correct (adjective)

2. In her left hand, she holds a tablet with the date July 4, 1776.

    ( )a. a pill, medicine (noun)
    ( )b. something to write on, made of stone (noun)

3. In her left hand, she holds a tablet with the date July 4, 1776.

    ( )a. a particular month, day, and year (noun)
    ( )b. a social appointment (noun)

4. Her full name is "Liberty Enlightening the World."

    ( )a. not hungry (adjective)
    ( )b. complete (adjective)

Vocabulary Practice

A. Write the correct word on each line below. Try to guess what the items are from the story you just read.

island	torch	visitor	pedestal	statue	tablet	crown

B. Fill in each blank with the correct word.

boxes	symbol	hand	island
lonely	tall	visitor	copper
size	monument	torch	arrive
tablets	date	crown	

1. The heart is a _____ of love.

2. He is 2 meters. That's very _____.

3. A penny isn't silver; it's _____.

4. A king wears a _____ on his head.

5. He bought three _____ of candy.

6. That statue is a national _____.

7. Maui is an _____ in Hawaii.

8. A _____ with the Olympic flame is carried from Greece for the Olympics.

9. Her _____ of birth is February 17, 1950.

10. Raise your _____ if you have any questions.

11. What _____ shoe do you wear?

12. He came to this country for only two months. He is a _____.

13. She is very old and she lives alone. She is very _____.

14. When will the letter _____?

15. The words were written on stone _____.

Word Forms

A. Choose the correct word form for each sentence.

1. *visit*　　*visitor*
   (verb)　　(noun)

   a. He doesn't live here. He's a _____.

   b. They _____ their parents every weekend.

2. *live*　　*life*　　*alive*　　*lively*
   (verb)　(noun)　(adjective)　(adjective)

   a. He has a good _____.

   b. They _____ in the U.S.

   c. That dog is very _____.

   d. Is the man dead or _____?

3. *arrive*　*arrival*
   (verb)　(noun)

   a. They are waiting for the _____ of the President.

   b. He is going to _____ at 6:00.

4. *immigrate*　　*immigrant*　　*immigration*
   (verb)　　　(noun)　　　(adjective)

   a. It is not easy to _____ to the U.S. at the present time.

   b. He is an Italian _____.

   c. Send your papers to the _____ office.

5. *free*   *freedom*   *free*   *freely*
   (verb)   (noun)   (adjective)   (adverb)

   a. Many people came to the New World for religious_____.

   b. This is a _____ country. You can say what you
      want.

   c. In some countries, you can't speak _____.

   d. The Emancipation Proclamation was written to _____
      the slaves in the U.S.

B. Choose the correct word form for each sentence.

1. *loneliness*   *lonely*   *alone*
   (noun)   (adjective)   (adjective)

   a. She is afraid to live _____.

   b. _____ is a problem in many big cities.

   c. He doesn't have any friends here. He is very_____.

2. *beauty*   *beautiful*
   (noun)   (adjective)

   a. She is a _____ baby.

   b. He wrote a poem about her _____.

3. *gold*   *gold*   *golden*
   (noun)   (adjective)   (adjective)

   a. _____ is very expensive.

   b. The _____ Gate Bridge is in San Francisco.

   c. She gave him a _____ ring.

4. *nation*   *national*
   (noun)   (adjective)

a. The U.S. is a young _____.

b. The _____ song of the U.S. is called "The Star Spangled Banner."

Prepositions

A. Write the correct preposition in each blank.

beside	from	in	of	on	to	with

She lives alone _____ an island, but she isn't lonely. She has

                1

visitors all the time. They come _____ admire her beauty and her

                2

size. She is very tall—ninety-two meters. _____ her right hand, she

                3

holds a torch. _____ her left hand, she holds a tablet _____

       4   5

the date July 4, 1776. She wears a copper crown.

She came _____ America _____ France _____ 1885.

        6   7   8

She arrived _____ New York _____ many boxes. It was a big

        9   10

job _____ put her together. It took one year.

    11

She stands _____ a pedestal made _____ America.

        12   13

_____ the base _____ the pedestal, it says, "... I lift my

  14   15

lamp _____ the golden door." She welcomes immigrants and visitors

     16

_____ this land.

  17

She is a national monument and a symbol _____ freedom. She is
18
the Statue of Liberty. Her full name is "Liberty Enlightening the World."

B. Read the story out loud, whispering the one-syllable prepositions.

Numbers

A. Write the words for the numbers. (These numbers are in the story.)

1. 92 _____

2. 1 _____

B. Write the numbers for the words. (These numbers are in the story.)

1. four _____

2. seventeen seventy-six _____

3. eighteen eighty-five _____

Make a Sentence

Choose one subject, one verb, and one object to make a complete sentence.
Draw lines to connect the parts of your sentences. One sentence has been
made for you.

Subject	*Verb*	*Object/Complement*
1. The Statue of Liberty	is	France.
2. It	welcomes	"Liberty Enlightening the World."
3. The date on the tablet	is	a symbol of freedom.
4. The statue	came from	very tall.
5. The Statue of Liberty	is	a national monument.
6. It	is	a torch and a tablet.
7. It	holds	July 4, 1776.
8. The statue's full name	is	immigrants and visitors.

Creative Writing

Write a message on this postcard to a friend in the United States.

The Statue of Liberty

Place Postage Here

Controlled Writing

Imagine that you are the Statue of Liberty. Rewrite the story on page 17
but change "she" to "I." Make any other changes that are necessary.

I live alone on an island, but I'm not lonely.

_____

_____

_____

_____

_____

_____

_____

_____

_____

_____

_____

_____

_____

_____

_____

_____

Dialogue and Improvisation

Fill in the missing parts of the dialogue. Work with a partner. Read the dialogue to the class.

A.
    —Where were you yesterday?
    —I went to see the Statue of Liberty.
    —What does it look like?
    —It's a _____.
    —Is it true that there are stairs inside the statue?
    —Yes, they go all the way up to the crown.
    —Did you walk up?
    —No, _____.
    —Oh, you're _____.

B.
    —I went to see the Statue of Liberty today.
    —How was it?
    —Great. Did you know the Statue of Liberty was a gift from the people of France?
    —Really? You mean _____?
    —Yes, then it was sent to America.
    —What about the pedestal?
    —Oh, the pedestal _____.

Chunking

A. Put a slash after each chunk in the story below. The first two sentences are marked for you. Look at the rules for chunking on page 13, if necessary.
B. Read the story silently. Read in chunks, not word by word.
C. Read the story out loud to the class. Remember, read in chunks.

She lives alone / on an island, / but she isn't lonely. / She has visitors / all the time. / They come to admire her beauty and her size. She is very tall—ninety-two meters. In her right hand, she holds a torch. In her left hand, she holds a tablet with the date July 4, 1776. She wears a copper crown.

She came to America from France in 1885. She arrived in New York in many boxes. It was a big job to put her together. It took one year.

She stands on a pedestal made in America. On the base of the pedestal, it says, ". . . I lift my lamp beside the golden door." She welcomes immigrants and visitors to this land.

She is a national monument and a symbol of freedom. She is the Statue of Liberty. Her full name is "Liberty Enlightening the World."

Vocabulary List

The following words are listed as they appear in the story. The dictionary form is given in parentheses. Read the words out loud. Pay attention to the stress and the number of syllables in each word.

Adjectives	*Nouns*	*Verbs*	*Adverbs*
lóne·ly	ís·land	lives (live)	a·lóne
tall	vís·i·tors (visitor)	come	vér·y
níne·ty	béau·ty	ad·míre	a·gáin
two	size	holds (hold)	
right	mé·ters (meter)	wears (wear)	
left	hand	came (come)	
cóp·per	torch	ar·ríved (arrive)	
one	táb·let	stood (stand)	
gól·den	date	stands (stand)	
ná·tion·al	Ju·lý	says (say)	
full	crown	lift	
en·líght·en·ing	A·mér·i·ca	wél·comes	
	France	(welcome)	
	píec·es (piece)		
	year		
	life		
	place		
	péd·es·tal		
	cóun·try		
	base		
	lamp		
	door		
	New Yórk		
	hár·bor		
	ímm·i·grants (immigrant)		
	món·u·ment		
	sým·bol		
	frée·dom		
	name		
	lí·ber·ty		
	world		
	stát·ue		

Thomas Jefferson

3

The Stars
and Stripes

A long time ago, England had thirteen colonies in America. These colonies had the same flag as England. After the Revolutionary War (1775–1783), the colonies became an independent country called the United States of America. The new country needed a new flag.

Betsy Ross, a Philadelphia dressmaker, made the first United States flag. She used the same colors as the English flag—red, white, and blue—but her design was different. Betsy Ross's flag had red and white stripes and thirteen white stars on a blue square. Each star represented one state. This became the official flag of the U.S.A. on June 14, 1777.*

The young country grew. There were more and more states. The last two states were Alaska and Hawaii. Today, the United States flag has fifty white stars—one for each state. This flag has thirteen red and white stripes. The stripes represent the thirteen original states. Americans call their flag "the Stars and Stripes."

159 words

* June 14 is Flag Day in the U.S.

Comprehension Questions

A. Answer true or false.

1. England had thirteen colonies in America. _____

2. The thirteen English colonies became the United States of America.

   _____

3. The colonies became independent before the Revolutionary War.

   _____

4. Betsy Ross made the first English flag. _____

5. The first U.S. flag was red, white, and blue. _____

6. Today, the United States has thirteen states. _____

B. Write the answers "Yes, it did" or "No, it didn't."

1. Did England have thirty colonies in America?

   _____

2. Did Betsy Ross's flag become the official United States flag?

   _____

3. Did the United States grow?

   _____

4. Did the United States have fifty states in 1777?

   _____

Inference Questions

Answer true or false.

1. The flag of England has stars and stripes. _____

2. The Revolutionary War was a war between the colonies and England.

   _____

3. The United States has been an independent country for more than 200

years. _____

Words with More Than One Meaning

Mark the answer that gives the correct meaning of the underlined word in each sentence.

1. The new country needed a new flag.

    ( )a. a nation, land (noun)
    ( )b. a place outside the city (noun)

2. Betsy Ross's flag had red and white stripes and thirteen white stars on a blue square.

    ( )a. an open public place (noun)
    ( )b. a figure with four equal sides (noun)

3. Each star represented one state.

    ( )a. a figure with five or six points (noun)
    ( )b. a famous actor or actress (noun)

Vocabulary Practice

Fill in each blank with the correct word.

flag	dressmaker	design
square	stars	represents
young	England	stripes
colors	different	

1. London is the capital of _____.

2. On June 14, my parents hang a _____ outside their house.

3. America is only 200 years old. It is a _____ country.

4. A flag _____ a country.

5. She works as a _____ for a clothing company.

6. He likes bright _____.

7. He won a prize for the best _____.

8. His shirt has blue and white _____.

9. Last night, there were many _____ in the sky.

10. A _____ has four equal sides.

11. They are brothers, but they are very _____.

Word Forms
Choose the correct word form for each sentence.

1. *independence*   *independent*
   (noun)   (adjective)

   a. The United States is an _____ country.

   b. Many countries are fighting for their _____.

2. *color*   *colorful*
   (noun)   (adjective)

   a. What is your favorite _____?

   b. That's a very _____ dress.

3. *difference*   *different*
   (noun)   (adjective)

   a. They speak _____ languages.

   b. What is the _____ between bread and toast?

4. *represent*   *representative*
   (verb)   (noun)

   a. An ambassador is a _____ of his or her country.

   b. What does a heart _____?

5. *England*   *English*   *English*
   (noun)   (noun)   (adjective)

  a. _____ is a small country.

  b. She speaks _____ perfectly.

  c. The _____ language is not easy to learn.

Prepositions

A. Write the correct preposition in each blank.

after   for   in   of   on

   A long time ago, England had thirteen colonies _____ America.
1
These colonies had the same flag as England. _____ the Revolution-
2
ary War (1775–1783), the colonies became an independent country called
the United States _____ America. The new country needed a new
3
flag.

   Betsy Ross, a Philadelphia dressmaker, made the first United States flag.
She used the same colors as the English flag—red, white, and blue—but
her design was different. Betsy Ross's flag had red and white stripes and
thirteen white stars _____ a blue square. Each star represented one
4
state. This became the official flag _____ the U.S.A. _____
5 **6**
June 14, 1777.

   The young country grew. There were more and more states. The last two
states were Alaska and Hawaii. Today, the United States flag has fifty
white stars—one _____ each state. This flag has thirteen red and
7

white stripes. The stripes represent the thirteen original states. Americans call their flag "the Stars and Stripes."

B. Read the story out loud, whispering the one-syllable prepositions.

Numbers

A. Write the words for the numbers. (These numbers are in the story.)

1. 13 _____

2. 1st _____

3. 2 _____

4. 50 _____

B. Write the numbers for the words. (These numbers are in the story.)

1. seventeen seventy-five _____

2. fourteen _____

3. seventeen seventy-seven _____

4. seventeen eighty-three _____

Make a Sentence

Choose one subject, one verb, and one object to make a complete sentence. Draw lines to connect the parts of your sentences.

Subject	*Verb*	*Object/Complement*
1. England	became	the U.S. flag.
2. The colonies	made	a new flag.
3. The new country	had	one state.
4. Betsy Ross	had	independent.
5. Betsy Ross's flag	represented	the first U.S. flag.
6. Each star	has	fifty states.
7. The United States	needed	thirteen colonies.
8. The U.S. flag	is	stars and stripes.
9. The Stars and Stripes	has	fifty stars.

Creative Writing

The flag of the United States is on the left. The flag of England is on the right. Write a comparison of the two flags, telling how they are alike and how they are different.

The Stars and Stripes

The Union Jack

_____

_____

_____

_____

_____

_____

_____

_____

_____

_____

_____

Dialogue and Improvisation

Fill in the missing parts of the dialogue. Work with a partner. Read the dialogue to the class.

A.
—Why are there flags everywhere today?
—It's Flag Day.

—Why is Flag Day on June 14?
—Because _____.
—In what year?
—In 1777.
—Was the flag the same in 1777?
—No, it had _____.
—Why is the flag different now?
—Because _____.

B.

—Is Flag Day a big holiday in America?
—What do you mean?
—Is it a national holiday like July 4 or _____?
—Not really.
—Do people work on Flag Day?
—Yes, they do.
—Are the banks and post offices open?
—Yes, and so are _____.
—So it's not a big holiday.
—No, but _____.

Chunking

A. Put a slash after each chunk in the story below. The first two sentences
   are marked for you. Look at the rules for chunking on page 13, if
   necessary.
B. Read the story silently. Read in chunks, not word by word.
C. Read the story out loud to the class. Remember, read in chunks.

A long time ago,   /   England had thirteen colonies   /   in America.   /
These colonies   /   had the same flag as England.   /   After the Revolutionary War (1775–1783), the colonies became an independent country
called the United States of America. The new country needed a new flag.

Betsy Ross, a Philadelphia dressmaker, made the first United States flag.
She used the same colors as the English flag—red, white, and blue—but
her design was different. Betsy Ross's flag had red and white stripes and
thirteen white stars on a blue square. Each star represented one state. This
became the official flag of the U.S.A. on June 14, 1777.

The young country grew. There were more and more states. The last two
states were Alaska and Hawaii. Today, the United States flag has fifty
white stars—one for each state. This flag has thirteen red and white stripes.
The stripes represent the thirteen original states. Americans call their flag
"the Stars and Stripes."

Vocabulary List

The following words are listed as they appear in the story. The dictionary form is given in parentheses. Read the words out loud. Pay attention to the stress and the number of syllables in each word.

Adjectives	*Nouns*	*Verbs*	*Adverbs*
long	time	néed·ed	a·gó
same	Éng·land	(need)	to·dáy
Rev·o·lú·tion·ar·y	thír·teén	made (make)	
in·de·pénd·ent	cól·o·nies (colony)	used (use)	
U·nít·ed	flag	rep·re·sént·ed	
new	war	(represent)	
Phil·a·dél·phi·a	States (state)	grew (grow)	
first	Bét·sy	rep·re·sént	
díf·ferent	Ross		
each	dréss·mak·er		
of·fí·cial	cól·ors (color)		
young	red		
more	white		
last	blue		
Éng·lish	de·sígn		
fíf·ty	stripes (stripe)		
o·ríg·i·nal	star		
white	square		
blue	June		
	A·lás·ka		
	Ha·wái·i		
	one		
	A·mér·i·cans		
	(American)		

4

Uncle Sam

Every American has the same uncle—Uncle Sam. He has long white hair and whiskers. He wears a top hat, coat, vest, and striped pants. How did everybody get the same uncle?

In the early 1800s, there was a businessman in upstate New York. His name was Samuel Wilson. He was friendly, and people called him "Uncle Sam." Uncle Sam was in the meat business. He sold meat to the United States army. He always wrote "U.S." on his boxes of meat. What did "U.S." mean—Uncle Sam or United States?

American soldiers ate Uncle Sam's meat. They began to call the U.S. government "Uncle Sam." Soon, there were cartoons about Uncle Sam in the newspapers. His picture became popular. During World War I, there was a famous poster* with a picture of Uncle Sam. Uncle Sam pointed his finger and said, "I WANT YOU FOR U.S. ARMY."

After this poster, everybody called the U.S. government "Uncle Sam." Some people didn't believe there really was an Uncle Sam Wilson. But in 1961, Congress said officially that the name "Uncle Sam" came from Samuel Wilson.

184 words

* Drawn by James Montgomery Flagg.

41

Comprehension Questions

A. Answer true or false.

1. Samuel Wilson was a friendly person. _____

2. People called Samuel Wilson "Uncle Sam." _____

3. Samuel Wilson was in the army. _____

4. Samuel Wilson sold meat to the U.S. army. _____

5. Samuel Wilson wrote "Uncle Sam" on his boxes of meat. _____

6. Soldiers called the U.S. government "Samuel Wilson." _____

B. Write the answers "Yes, he did" or "Yes, it did," or "No, he didn't" or "No, it didn't."

1. Did Samuel Wilson live in New York City?

   _____

2. Did the poster with Uncle Sam's picture become famous?

   _____

3. Did Congress say that the name "Uncle Sam" came from Samuel Wilson?

   _____

Inference Questions

Answer true or false.

1. "Uncle Sam" represents the U.S. government. _____

2. A poster with a picture of Uncle Sam was used by the army.

   _____

3. Samuel Wilson really wore a top hat, coat, vest, and striped pants.

_____

Skimming

A. Find all the *names* for Sam that are in the story. Write each name on the lines below. Don't read the story again—just look for the names.

_____*Sam*_____   _____

_____   _____

B. Find all the *clothes* in the story.

_____   _____

_____   _____

C. Find the *years* in the story.

_____   _____

Words with More Than One Meaning

Mark the answer that gives the correct meaning of the underlined word in each sentence.

1. Soon, there were <u>cartoons</u> in the newspapers about Uncle Sam.

( )a. a drawing on paper, usually funny (noun)
( )b. animated drawings on television or in movies (noun)

2. His <u>picture</u> became popular.

( )a. photograph (noun)
( )b. image, likeness (noun)

Vocabulary Practice

A. Write the correct word on each line below. Don't use your dictionary. Try to guess what the items are from the story you just read.

B. Fill in each blank with the correct word.

boxes	upstate	meat	army
popular	coat	uncle	picture
cartoon	vest	pants	soldiers
point	Congress	posters	believe

1. A man's suit has a jacket and _____.

2. My mother's brother is my _____.

3. A three-piece suit has a jacket, pants, and a _____.

4. When it's cold outside, you need to wear a _____.

5. She doesn't live in New York City, she lives in _____ New York.

6. Beef is one kind of _____.

7. He doesn't want to join the navy; he wants to join the _____.

8. Before we moved to a new apartment we put all our books in _____.

9. People in the army are called _____.

10. There was a funny _____ about the President in the newspaper yesterday.

11. Can you draw a _____ of yourself?

12. Everybody likes her. She is very _____.

13. He has many _____ of rock singers on his walls.

14. Please don't _____ your finger at me.

15. I don't _____ you're thirty-five years old!

16. He is a senator from California. He is a member of _____.

Word Forms

Choose the correct word form for each sentence.

1. *business*   *businessman*
   (noun)   (noun)

   a. He is not an artist, he's a _____.

   b. What kind of _____ are you in?

2. *name*   *name*
   (verb)   (noun)

   a. They are going to _____ the baby John.

   b. What's your _____?

3. *friend*   *friendly*
   (noun)   (adjective)

   a. He has only one good _____.

   b. She's a very _____ person.

4. *mean*   *meaning*
   (verb)   (noun)

   a. What does "cartoon" _____?

   b. Do you know the _____ of "cartoon"?

5. *begin*   *beginning*
   (verb)   (noun)

   a. What time does the movie _____?

   b. Many people came to America at the _____ of the
   twentieth century.

6. *governor*   *government*
   (noun)   (noun)

   a. The U.S. _____ is in Washington, D.C.

   b. Nelson A. Rockefeller was the _____ of New York
   State three times.

7. *office*   *official*   *officially*
   (noun)   (adjective)   (adverb)

   a. She needs an _____ letter from her consulate.

   b. He works in an _____ on the tenth floor.

   c. The President said it _____.

Prepositions

A. Write the correct preposition in each blank.

about	after	during	for	from	in	of	on	to	with

Every American has the same uncle—Uncle Sam. He has long white hair and whiskers. He wears a top hat, coat, vest, and striped pants. How did everybody get the same uncle?

_____ the early 1800s, there was a businessman _____
    1   2
upstate New York. His name was Samuel Wilson. He was friendly, and people called him "Uncle Sam." Uncle Sam was _____ the meat
                                                                  3
business. He sold meat _____ the United States army. He always
                            4
wrote "U.S." _____ his boxes _____ meat. What did "U.S."
                  5   6
mean—Uncle Sam or United States?

American soldiers ate Uncle Sam's meat. They began _____ call
                                                          7
the U.S. government "Uncle Sam." Soon, there were cartoons _____
                                                                8
Uncle Sam _____ the newspapers. His picture became popular.
              9

_____ World War I, there was a famous poster _____ a picture
    10   11
_____ Uncle Sam. Uncle Sam pointed his finger and said, "I WANT
    12
YOU _____ U.S. ARMY."
         13

_____ this poster, everybody called the U.S. government "Uncle
    14
Sam." Some people didn't believe there really was an Uncle Sam Wilson.
But _____ 1961, Congress said officially that the name "Uncle Sam"
        15
came _____ Samuel Wilson.
        16

B. Read the story out loud, whispering the one-syllable prepositions.

Numbers

Write the numbers for the words. (These numbers are in the story.)

1. the eighteen hundreds ⎯⎯⎯⎯⎯⎯

2. nineteen sixty-one ⎯⎯⎯⎯⎯⎯

Make a Sentence

Choose one subject, one verb, and one object to make a complete sentence. Draw lines to connect the parts of your sentences.

Subject	*Verb*	*Object/Complement*
1. Every American	used	a businessman.
2. He	wears	the U.S. government "Uncle Sam."
3. Samuel Wilson	sold	the same uncle.
4. He	ate	a poster with a picture of Uncle Sam.
5. Soldiers	became	Uncle Sam's meat.
6. The army	called	a vest and striped pants.
7. Uncle Sam's picture	has	meat.
8. Everybody	came from	Samuel Wilson.
9. The name "Uncle Sam"	was	popular.

Creative Writing

This is the original poster of Uncle Sam, drawn by James Montgomery Flagg. Write a paragraph describing the poster and explaining what it means.

_____

_____

_____

_____

_____

_____

_____

_____

_____

_____

_____

_____

_____

_____

_____

_____

Dialogue and Improvisation

Fill in the missing parts of the dialogue. Work with a partner. Read the dialogue to the class.

—Look at this paycheck. Uncle Sam took 30 percent of my salary!
—Why did he do that?
—He uses the money for the military.
—Your uncle must be a big man.
—What uncle?
—Your Uncle Sam.
—Uncle Sam isn't my real uncle. It's _____
_____.

—Why do you call the U.S. government Uncle Sam?
—Because _____.
—Oh, I _____.

Chunking

A. Put a slash after each chunk in the story below. The first two sentences are marked for you. Look at the rules for chunking on page 13, if necessary.
B. Read the story silently. Read in chunks, not word by word.
C. Read the story out loud to the class. Remember, read in chunks.

   Every American / has the same uncle— / Uncle Sam. / He has long white hair and whiskers. / He wears a top hat, coat, vest, and striped pants. How did everybody get the same uncle?

In the early 1800s, there was a businessman in upstate New York. His name was Samuel Wilson. He was friendly, and people called him "Uncle Sam." Uncle Sam was in the meat business. He sold meat to the United States army. He always wrote "U.S." on his boxes of meat. What did "U.S." mean—Uncle Sam or United States?

American soldiers ate Uncle Sam's meat. They began to call the U.S. government "Uncle Sam." Soon, there were cartoons about Uncle Sam in the newspapers. His picture became popular. During World War I, there was a famous poster with a picture of Uncle Sam. Uncle Sam pointed his finger and said, "I WANT YOU FOR U.S. ARMY."

After this poster, everybody called the U.S. government "Uncle Sam." Some people didn't believe there really was an Uncle Sam Wilson. But in 1961, Congress said officially that the name "Uncle Sam" came from Samuel Wilson.

Vocabulary List

The following words are listed as they appear in the story. The dictionary form is given in parentheses. Read the words out loud. Pay attention to the stress and the number of syllables in each word.

Adjectives	*Nouns*	*Nouns*	*Verbs*
év·ery	A·mér·i·can	búsi·ness	wears (wear)
same	ún·cle	meat	get
long	Sam	ár·my	sold (sell)
white	hair	bóx·es (box)	mean
top	whísk·ers (whisker)	sól·diers (soldier)	ate (eat)
striped	hat	góv·ern·ment	be·gán (begin)
eár·ly	coat	car·toóns (cartoon)	call
up·státe	vest	néws·pa·pers	póint·ed (point)
friénd·ly	pants	(newspaper)	said (say)
meat	búsi·ness·man	píc·ture	want
A·mér·i·can	name	póst·er	be·liéve
póp·u·lar	Sám·u·el	fín·ger	cáme from
world	Wíl·son	Cóng·ress	(come)
fá·mous			

Adverbs

ál·ways
soon
of·fí·cial·ly
réal·ly

CENTRAL
WASHINGTON, D.C.

5

1600 Pennsylvania Avenue, Washington, D.C.

The white house at 1600 Pennsylvania Avenue is not an ordinary house. The President of the United States lives there.

The White House is a three-story building, with columns in the front and back. It has 107 rooms. One of them is the famous Oval Office. The building was made of limestone, a gray stone. Later, it was painted white.

The architect for the President's house was James Hoban. Hoban immigrated to the United States from Ireland. At that time, in America, there was an architecture competition. Hoban won the competition. He got $500, a piece of land in Washington, D.C., and the chance to design the President's house.

Work began in 1792 and ended in 1800. But during the War of 1812, the British army burned the building. The President's house was destroyed. Hoban helped rebuild the White House after the war.

There is another white house* in a quiet section of Dublin, Ireland. It looks very much like the one in Washington. People think this house is a copy of the White House in Washington. But the fact is that the house in Dublin was built in 1745.

Maybe the White House at 1600 Pennsylvania Avenue is not the most original white house in the world, but it is probably the most famous.

216 words

* Leinster House.

Comprehension Questions

A. Answer true or false.

1. The President's house has 107 rooms. _____

2. James Hoban designed the President's house. _____

3. The White House is at 1600 Washington Avenue. _____

4. The White House is a five-story building. _____

5. The President of the U.S. lives in Washington, D.C. _____

6. The President asked Hoban to design the White House. _____

7. It took eight years to build the White House. _____

8. The White House is a famous building. _____

B. Write the answer "Yes, it was" or "No, it wasn't."

1. Was the President's house painted white?

_____

2. Was the White House burned by the British?

_____

3. Was the White House rebuilt before the War of 1812?

_____

4. Was the white house in Ireland built in 1792?

_____

5. Was the White House built in Pennsylvania?

_____

Inference Questions

Answer true or false.

1. Hoban probably used the white house in Dublin as a model for his

   design. _____

2. The Oval Office is the Vice President's office. _____

3. The White House is a small house. _____

4. The President's house is called the "White House" because it was painted

   white. _____

Skimming

Find all the *years* in the story and write them on the lines below. Don't read the story again, just look for the years.

_____   _____   _____   _____

Words with More Than One Meaning

Mark the answer that gives the correct meaning of the underlined word in each sentence.

1. The White House is a three-story building, with <u>columns</u> in the front and back.

   ( )a. upright supports (noun)
   ( )b. vertical sections of a printed page (noun)

2. The White House is a three-story building, with columns in the front and <u>back</u>.

   ( )a. the rear part of the body (noun)
   ( )b. the rear of a building (noun)

3. But during the War of 1812, the British army <u>burned</u> the building.

   ( )a. destroyed by fire (verb)
   ( )b. injured by heat (verb)

4. People think this house is a <u>copy</u> of the White House in Washington.

( )a. to write the same answer, to cheat (verb)
( )b. a reproduction, an imitation (noun)

Vocabulary Practice

Fill in each blank with the correct word.

army	house	President
story	white	section
Ordinary	War	front
actress		

1. She has very _____ teeth.

2. When he was in the _____ he was in Vietnam.

3. Katharine Hepburn is a famous American _____.

4. After they get married, they are going to buy a _____.

5. He lives in a nice _____ of New Jersey.

6. Hiroshima was destroyed during World _____ II.

7. George Washington was the first _____ of the United States.

8. The World Trade Center is a 110-_____ building.

9. The _____ door is locked.

10. Did you see the movie "_____ People"?

Word Forms

Choose the correct word form for each sentence.

1. *build*   *rebuild*   *building*
   (verb)   (verb)   (noun)

   a. The _____ was made of stone.

b. They want to _____ a house in Texas.

c. After the fire, they started to _____ their house.

2. *paint*　　*paint*　　*painting*
   (verb)　　(noun)　　(noun)

   a. Be careful, that's wet _____.

   b. Jasper Johns, an American artist, made a _____

   of the U.S. flag.

   c. He is going to _____ his bedroom.

3. *architect*　　*architecture*
   (noun)　　　(noun)

   a. She is studying to be an _____.

   b. Do you like modern _____?

4. *compete*　　*competition*
   (verb)　　　(noun)

   a. The U.S. didn't _____ in the 1980 Olympics in

   the Soviet Union.

   b. There is a lot of _____ for the job.

5. *win*　　*winner*
   (verb)　　(noun)

   a. He didn't _____ the race.

   b. The _____ of the contest was very happy.

6. *design*　　*designer*
   (verb)　　(noun)

   a. Calvin Klein is an American fashion _____.

   b. He can _____ both men's and women's clothes.

Prepositions

A. Write the correct preposition in each blank.

after	at	during	for	from	in	of	to	with

The white house _____ 1600 Pennsylvania Avenue is not an ordinary house. The President _____ the United States lives there.

The White House is a three-story building, _____ columns _____ the front and back. It has 107 rooms. One _____ them is the famous Oval Office. The building was made _____ limestone, a gray stone. Later, it was painted white.

The architect _____ the President's house was James Hoban. Hoban immigrated _____ the United States _____ Ireland. _____ that time, _____ America, there was an architecture competition. Hoban won the competition. He got $500, a piece _____ land _____ Washington, D.C., and the chance _____ design the President's house.

Work began _____ 1792 and ended _____ 1800. But _____ the War _____ 1812, the British army burned the building. The President's house was destroyed. Hoban helped rebuild the White House _____ the war.

There is another white house _____ a quiet section _____ Dublin, Ireland. It looks very much like the one _____ Washington. People think this house is a copy _____ the White House _____

Washington. But the fact is that the house _____ Dublin was built
                                              25

_____ 1745.
   26

Maybe the White House _____ 1600 Pennsylvania Avenue is not
                          27

the most original white house _____ the world, but it is probably
                                  28

the most famous.

B. Read the story out loud, whispering the one-syllable prepositions.

Numbers

Write the numbers for the words. (These numbers are in the story.)

1. sixteen hundred   _____

2. one hundred seven   _____

3. five hundred dollars   _____

4. seventeen ninety-two   _____

5. eighteen hundred   _____

6. eighteen twelve   _____

7. seventeen forty-five   _____

Make a Sentence

Choose one subject, one verb, and one object to make a complete sentence.
Draw lines to connect the parts of your sentences.

Subject	Verb	Object/Complement
1. The White House	is	limestone.
2. One room	was	the President's house.
3. The building	won	107 rooms.
4. The architect	has	a competition.
5. Hoban	is	the Oval Office.
6. He	designed	James Hoban.
7. The British Army	burned	the building.
8. The house at 1600 Pennsylvania Avenue	was made of	famous.

Creative Writing
Write a message on this postcard to a friend in the United States.

The White House

Place
Postage
Here

Controlled Writing

George Washington, the first President of the United States, didn't live in the White House. In fact, he was the only President who didn't live in the White House. He was President from 1789 to 1797, before the White House was completed. Washington lived in a house called Mount Vernon. Use the information below to write a story about Mount Vernon.

Mount Vernon

Fairfax County, Virginia
fifteen miles from Washington, D.C.
a two-story building
eight columns in the front
made of wood
painted white
built in the early 1700s
now a museum

_____

_____

_____

_____

Dialogue and Improvisation

Fill in the missing parts of the dialogue. Work with a partner. Read the dialogue to the class.

A.
    —What did you do this weekend?
    —I went to Washington, D.C.
    —What did you do there?
    —I saw the White House.
    —What does it look like?
    —It's a _____.
    —Did you go inside?
    —Yes.
    —What did you see?
    —_____.

B.
    —What did you do this weekend?
    —I went to Virginia.
    —Did you see Mount Vernon?
    —Yes, I did.
    —What does it look like?
    —It's a _____.
    —Oh, _____.

Chunking

A. Put a slash after each chunk in the story below. Try to read in bigger chunks. Short sentences should be only one chunk. The first two sentences are marked for you.

B. Read the story silently. Read in chunks, not word by word.

C. Read the story out loud to the class. Remember, read in chunks.

    The white house at 1600 Pennsylvania Avenue / is not / an ordinary house. / The President of the United States / lives there. /

The White House is a three-story building, with columns in the front and back. It has 107 rooms. One of them is the famous Oval Office. The building was made of limestone, a gray stone. Later, it was painted white.

The architect for the President's house was James Hoban. Hoban immigrated to the United States from Ireland. At that time, in America, there was an architecture competition. Hoban won the competition. He got $500, a piece of land in Washington, D.C., and the chance to design the President's house.

Work began in 1792 and ended in 1800. But during the War of 1812, the British army burned the building. The President's house was destroyed. Hoban helped rebuild the White House after the war.

There is another white house in a quiet section of Dublin, Ireland. It looks very much like the one in Washington. People think this house is a copy of the White House in Washington. But the fact is that the house in Dublin was built in 1745.

Maybe the White House at 1600 Pennsylvania Avenue is not the most original white house in the world, but it is probably the most famous.

Vocabulary List

The following words are listed as they appear in the story. The dictionary form is given in parentheses. Read the words out loud. Pay attention to the stress and the number of syllables in each word.

Adjectives	*Nouns*		*Verbs*
ór·di·nar·y	house	ár·chi·tect	páint·ed (paint)
thrée-stó·ry	Penn·syl·vá·nia	Íre·land	ím·mi·grat·ed
Ó·val	á·ve·nue	ár·chi·tec·ture	(immigrate)
gray	Prés·i·dent	com·pe·tí·tion	won (win)
Brít·ish	buíld·ing	piece	got (get)
quí·et	cól·umns	Wásh·ing·ton	de·sígn
o·ríg·i·nal	(column)	chance	énd·ed (end)
	front	work	burned (burn)
	back	séc·tion	de·stróyed (destroy)
Adverbs	rooms (room)	Dúb·lin	helped (help)
there	óf·fice	cóp·y	re·buíld
máy·be	líme·stone	fact	looks (look)
most	stone		think
prób·a·bly			built (build)

6

The First Oil Well in the World

Titusville, Pennsylvania is not New York or Washington, but it is still a historic place. In 1859, a man named Edwin Drake drilled for oil in Titusville. This was the first successful oil well in the world.

For hundreds of years, people used oil for lighting purposes and medical purposes. They got this oil from seepages—small openings in the ground. This oil came out of the ground by itself. But drilling for oil was something completely new. Drake's invention started the oil industry.

The modern world needed oil for everyday life. Drake's drilling method became very popular. By the end of the 1800s, oil was discovered in fourteen states. The United States became the largest oil exporter in the world.

There is a saying that all good things come to an end. Now, the U.S. imports about half of its oil. In fact, the United States is the largest oil importer in the world.

For Edwin Drake, all good things came to an end too. Drake never got a patent on his drilling method. He didn't make any money from his invention. He even lost money in the oil business. He lived a very poor life. Finally, the Pennsylvania government gave him a pension. Drake died a poor man twenty-one years after his historic, billion-dollar invention.

219 words

Comprehension Questions

A. Answer true or false.

1. Edwin Drake drilled the first successful oil well. _____

2. The first successful oil well was in Washington. _____

3. People drilled for oil hundreds of years ago. _____

4. A seepage is a small opening in the ground. _____

5. Between 1859 and 1900, oil was discovered in fourteen states. _____

6. The modern world didn't need oil. _____

7. At first, the U.S. was the largest oil importer. _____

8. Later, the U.S. became the largest oil exporter. _____

9. Drake died a poor man. _____

B. Write the answer "Yes, he did" or "No, he didn't."

1. Did Drake drill for oil in Titusville, Pennsylvania?

   _____

2. Did Drake find oil?

   _____

3. Did Drake make money in the oil business?

   _____

4. Did Drake get a patent?

   _____

Inference Questions

Answer true or false.

1. Titusville is a big city like New York. _____

2. Many countries import oil. _____

3. To make money from an invention, you need a patent on it.

   _____

4. Drake's drilling method was used in many states. _____

Skimming

Find all the *place names* (city, state, country) in the story and write them on the lines below. Don't read the story again—just look for the place names.

_____*Titusville*_____   _____

_____   _____

_____

Synonyms

Write a synonym (a word with similar meaning) for each word below. The synonyms are in the story.

1. industry   = _____*business*_____

2. seepages = _____

3. famous   = _____

4. biggest   = _____

5. expression = _____

Antonyms

Write an antonym (a word with the opposite meaning) for each word below. The antonyms are in the story.

1. old   _____*new*_____

2. unpopular   _____

3. exporter   _____

4. bad   _____

5. beginning   _____

6. exports   _____

7. smallest   _____

8. lived   _____

9. rich   _____

10. last   _____

11. unsuccessful   _____

Words with More Than One Meaning

Mark the answer that gives the correct meaning of the underlined word in each sentence.

1. In 1859, a man named Edwin Drake <u>drilled</u> for oil in Titusville.

   ( )a. made a hole (verb)
   ( )b. practiced, exercised (verb)

2. This was the first successful oil <u>well</u> in the world.

   ( )a. hole in the ground (noun)
   ( )b. fine, good (adverb)

3. But drilling for <u>oil</u> was something new.

   ( )a. petroleum (noun)
   ( )b. a vegetable substance for cooking (noun)

4. He even <u>lost</u> money in the oil business.

   ( )a. couldn't find (verb)
   ( )b. didn't earn (verb)

Vocabulary Practice

Fill in each blank with the correct word.

lost	billion	imports	poor
modern	medical	drilled	saying
exporter	historic	successful	ground
half	industry	Pennsylvania	largest
importer	patent	pension	oil

1. The dentist _____ a hole in my tooth.

2. Washington, the capital of the U.S., is a _____ place.

3. He earns a lot of money. He is a _____ business-man.

4. _____ is a state in the U.S.

5. When you go to the gas station, check the _____.

6. "M.D." means _____ doctor.

7. Many people have made money in the oil _____.

8. The little boy fell down on the _____.

9. Los Angeles is a _____ city.

10. Alaska is the _____ state in the U.S.

11. Her company sends fruit to other countries. She is an _____.

12. "Time is money" is an American _____.

13. The U.S. _____ cars from Japan.

14. Fifty percent is the same as _____.

15. Now, the U.S. is a big oil _____.

16. She got a _____ and made $1,000,000 on her invention.

17. He _____ money at the race track.

18. There are many _____ people in America.

19. In the United States, workers can get a _____ when they are sixty-two years old.

20. $5,000,000,000 is five _____ dollars.

Word Forms

Choose the correct word form for each sentence.

1. *history*   *historic*
   (noun)   (adjective)

   a. She is studying American _____ in college.

   b. Mount Vernon is a _____ house because George Washington lived there.

2. *drill*   *drill*
   (verb)   (noun)

   a. A dentist uses a _____.

   b. They plan to _____ for oil.

3. *oil*   *oily*
   (noun)   (adjective)

   a. The car needs _____.

   b. He has _____ skin.

4. *success*   *successful*
   (noun)   (adjective)

   a. She is a _____ lawyer.

   b. His invention was a big _____.

5. *light*   *light*   *lighting*
   (verb)   (noun)   (adjective)

   a. Please _____ my cigarette.

   b. Turn on the _____. It's dark in here.

   c. That store sells _____ fixtures.

6. *medicine*   *medical*
   (noun)   (adjective)

   a. Did you read this _____ report?

   b. He is studying _____.

7. *open*   *opening*
   (verb)   (noun)

   a. The _____ is on the other side.

   b. Please _____ the window.

8. *news*   *new*
   (noun)   (adjective)

   a. Is that a _____ coat?

   b. Did you hear today's _____?

9. *export*   *exporter*
   (verb)   (noun)

   a. He is an _____.

   b. Does his company _____ computers?

10. *say*   *saying*
    (verb)   (noun)

    a. "A penny saved is a penny earned" is a _____
       by Benjamin Franklin.

    b. What did you _____?

11. *import*   *importer*
    (verb)   (noun)

   a. Does your country _____ many products?

   b. He is a champagne _____.

12. *die*   *death*
    (verb)   (noun)

   a. Did George Washington _____ in 1799?

   b. John's _____ was a shock.

Prepositions

A. Write the correct preposition in each blank.

after	by	for	from	in	of	on	to

Titusville, Pennsylvania is not New York or Washington, but it is still a

historic place. _____ 1859, a man named Edwin Drake drilled
                    1

_____ oil _____ Titusville. This was the first successful oil
   2   3

well _____ the world.
       4

   For hundreds _____ years, people used oil _____ lighting
                    5   6

purposes and medical purposes. They got this oil _____ seepages—
                                                     7

small openings _____ the ground. This oil came out _____
                  8   9

the ground _____ itself. But drilling _____ oil was something
              10   11

completely new. Drake's invention started the oil industry.

   The modern world needed oil _____ everyday life. Drake's drilling
                                   12

method became very popular. _____ the end _____ the 1800s,

13   14

oil was discovered _____ fourteen states. The United States became

15

the largest oil exporter _____ the world.

16

   There is a saying that all good things come _____ an end. Now,

17

the U.S. imports about half _____ its oil. _____ fact, the

18   19

United States is the largest oil importer _____ the world.

20

_____ Edwin Drake, all good things came _____ an end

21   22

too. Drake never got a patent _____ his drilling method. He

23

didn't make any money _____ his invention. He even lost money

24

_____ the oil business. He lived a very poor life. Finally, the Penn-

25

sylvania government gave him a pension. Drake died a poor man twenty-

one years _____ his historic, billion-dollar invention.

26

B. Read the story out loud, whispering the one-syllable prepositions.

Numbers

A. Write the words for the numbers. (These numbers are in the story.)

   1. 1st   _____

   2. 21   _____

   3. $1,000,000,000   _____

B. Write the numbers for the words. (These numbers are in the story.)

   1. eighteen fifty-nine   · _____

   2. the eighteen hundreds   _____

Make a Sentence

Choose one subject, one verb, and one object to make a complete sentence. Write your sentences on the lines below.

Subject	*Verb*	*Object/Complement*
Titusville, Pennsylvania	was	oil.
Edwin Drake	started	a poor man.
Drilling for oil	lived	a patent.
Drake's discovery	became	a historic place.
Drake's drilling method	gave	the oil industry.
The U.S.	didn't make	any money.
Drake	is	him a pension.
He	imports	something new.
He	died	about half of its oil.
The Pennsylvania government	drilled for	a poor life.
Drake	never got	very popular.

1. _____

2. _____

3. _____

4. _____

5. _____

6. _____

7. _____

8. _____

9. _____

10. _____

11. _____

Creative Writing

The story in this chapter is about oil. Edwin Drake is part of the story. Write a story about Edwin Drake or a person like him.

Edwin Drake

_____

_____

_____

_____

_____

_____

_____

_____

_____

_____

_____

_____

_____

_____

_____

_____

Dialogue and Improvisation

Fill in the missing parts of the dialogue. Work with a partner. Read the dialogue to the class.

—Do you know who Edwin Drake is?
—No, I don't. Who is he?
—He _____.
—When?
—_____.
—Where?
—_____.
—I bet he got rich!
—No, _____.
—That's _____.

Chunking

A. Put a slash after each chunk in the story. Try to read in bigger chunks. Short sentences should be only one chunk. The first two sentences are marked for you.
B. Read the story silently. Read in chunks, not word by word.
C. Read the story out loud to the class. Remember, read in chunks.

Titusville, / Pennsylvania / is not New York or Washington, / but it is still a historic place. / In 1859, / a man named Edwin Drake drilled for oil in Titusville. / This was the first successful oil well in the world.

For hundreds of years, people used oil for lighting purposes and medical purposes. They got this oil from seepages—small openings in the ground. This oil came out of the ground by itself. But drilling for oil was something completely new. Drake's invention started the oil industry.

The modern world needed oil for everyday life. Drake's drilling method became very popular. By the end of the 1800s, oil was discovered in fourteen states. The United States became the largest oil exporter in the world.

There is a saying that all good things come to an end. Now, the U.S. imports about half of its oil. In fact, the United States is the largest oil importer in the world.

For Edwin Drake, all good things came to an end too. Drake never got a patent on his drilling method. He didn't make any money from his invention. He even lost money in the oil business. He lived a very poor life. Finally, the Pennsylvania government gave him a pension. Drake died a poor man twenty-one years after his historic, billion-dollar invention.

Vocabulary List

The following words are listed as they appear in the story. The dictionary form is given in parentheses. Read the words out loud. Pay attention to the stress and the number of syllables in each word.

Adjectives	*Nouns*	*Verbs*	*Adverbs*
his·tór·ic	Tí·tus·ville	named (name)	név·er
suc·céss·ful	place	drilled (drill)	é·ven
líght·ing	man	was used (use)	fí·nal·ly
méd·i·cal	Éd·win	came oút of (come)	
small	Drake	stárt·ed (start)	
mód·ern	oil	was dis·cóv·ered	
év·ery·dáy	óil wéll	(discover)	
dríll·ing	world	ím·ports (import)	
lárg·est (large)	púr·pos·es	lost (lose)	
oil	(purpose)	lived (live)	
good	séep·ag·es	gave (give)	
poor	(seepage)	died (die)	
Penn·syl·ván·ia	ó·pen·ings		
twén·ty·óne	(opening)		
bíl·lion-dól·lar	ground		
	dríll·ing (drill)		
	in·vén·tion		
	ín·dus·try		
	méth·od		
	ex·pórt·er		
	sáy·ing		
	end		
	half		
	im·pórt·er		
	pát·ent		
	pén·sion		
	man		
	years (year)		

7

Prohibition

The American Constitution guarantees freedom of speech, religion, and the press. In 1920, a new law (the Eighteenth Amendment) was added to the Constitution. This law said that Americans did not have the freedom to drink.

With a new law, there are often new crimes. Liquor stores, bars, and restaurants didn't sell alcohol. But some people wanted to drink. They drank in secret, illegal places. When they ordered drinks, they spoke softly. That's why such a place was called a "speakeasy."

It was illegal to make alcohol. Liquor companies were closed. But people made alcohol secretly, at night. This illegal alcohol was called "moonshine."

It was also illegal to sell or carry alcohol. When people sold alcohol, they carried the bottles in the leg of their boot. This crime was called "bootlegging."

The time when it was illegal to drink, to make, or to sell alcohol was called Prohibition. During Prohibition, gangsters controlled the liquor business. They organized the production of "moonshine" and sold it in their "speakeasies." It was a big business. "Bootlegging" got a new meaning. Gangsters transported liquor in cars, trucks, and ships.

Prohibition didn't stop people from drinking. But it added new crimes to American life. In 1933, Prohibition ended. A new law was added to the Constitution (the Twenty-first Amendment). It canceled the Eighteenth Amendment. This gave Americans the "freedom" to drink. What do you think about this freedom?

235 words

79

Comprehension Questions

A. Write the answer "Yes, it does" or "No, it doesn't."

1. Does the American Constitution guarantee freedom of speech, religion, and the press?

   _____

2. Does the Constitution guarantee the freedom to drink?

   _____

3. Does the American Constitution have amendments?

   _____

B. Write the answer "Yes, it/they did" or "No, it/they didn't."

1. Did the Twenty-first Amendment say that Americans did not have the freedom to drink?

   _____

2. Did the Twenty-first Amendment cancel the Eighteenth Amendment?

   _____

3. Did people make "moonshine" during Prohibition?

   _____

4. Did liquor companies make liquor during Prohibition?

   _____

5. Did people sell liquor illegally during Prohibition?

   _____

C. Write the answer to each question. Use the information given in the story.

1. *Who* controlled the liquor business during Prohibition?

   _____

2. *Where* did people go to drink during Prohibition?

_____

3. *How* did people order drinks during Prohibition?

_____

4. *What* was illegal liquor called during Prohibition?

_____

5. *How long* did Prohibition last in the U.S.?

_____

Inference Questions

Answer true or false.

1. New laws can be added to the American Constitution. _____

2. Prohibition was very successful. _____

3. Gangsters work in illegal businesses. _____

Skimming

A. Find the names of *places* in the story where people can buy liquor and write them on the lines below. Don't read the story again—just look for the place names.

_____   _____

_____   _____

B. Find the *crimes* in the story.

_____

_____

_____

C. Find the *freedoms* in the story.

_____   _____

_____   _____

Synonyms

Write a synonym for each word below. The synonyms are in the story.

1. liquor   = _____

2. produce = _____

3. carry   = _____

Antonyms

Write an antonym for each word below. The antonyms are in the story.

1. buy   _____

2. legal   _____

3. open   _____

4. small   _____

5. began   _____

Words with More Than One Meaning

Mark the answer that gives the correct meaning of the underlined word in each sentence.

1. The American Constitution guarantees freedom of speech, religion, and the press.
   ( )a. print and broadcast media (noun)
   ( )b. flatten, push (verb)

2. Liquor stores, bars, and restaurants didn't sell alcohol.
   ( )a. long, solid objects (noun)
   ( )b. places to drink alcohol (noun)

Vocabulary Practice

Fill in each blank with the correct word.

bottles	gangster	liquor
restaurant	alcohol	bar
law	freedom	drink
Prohibition	illegal	ended
religion	Amendment	press
ordered	crime	Constitution

1. The Nineteenth _____ to the Constitution gave women the right to vote.

2. Many people came to America for freedom of _____.

3. The President spoke to the _____ outside the White House.

4. In some countries, people do not have _____ of speech.

5. If she continues to _____, she will become an alcoholic.

6. It's against the _____ to smoke on public transportation.

7. Killing someone is a serious _____.

8. In some states, _____ stores are open on Sunday.

9. Every night after work, he goes to a _____ to have a few drinks.

10. She eats lunch in a _____ every day.

11. Heroin is an _____ drug.

12. They _____ hamburgers from the waiter.

13. She drinks Coke because she doesn't like the taste of _____.

14. She bought ten _____ of liquor for the party.

15. The laws of a country are in its _____.

16. Many movies were made about bootlegging during _____.

17. Al Capone was the most famous _____ during Prohibition.

18. Prohibition began in 1920 and _____ in 1933.

Word Forms

Choose the correct word form for each sentence.

1. *speak*   *speech*
   (verb)   (noun)

   a. They _____ a little English.

   b. Americans have freedom of _____.

2. *religion*   *religious*
   (noun)   (adjective)

   a. He is a very _____ person.

   b. She wants to change her _____.

3. *law*   *lawyer*   *legal*   *illegal*
   (noun)   (noun)   (adjective)   (adjective)

   a. You need a good _____.

   b. Drinking is not against the _____.

   c. It is _____ to carry a gun without a permit.

   d. Christmas is a _____ holiday in the U.S.

4. *drink*   *drink*   *drinking*
   (verb)   (noun)   (adjective)

   a. What do you _____ with your dinner?

   b. This is a strong _____.

   c. He has a _____ problem.

Prepositions

A. Write the correct preposition in each blank.

| about | at | during | from | in | of | to | with |

The American Constitution guarantees freedom _____ speech,

1

religion, and the press. _____ 1920, a new law (the Eighteenth

2

Amendment) was added _____ the Constitution. This law said that

3

Americans did not have the freedom _____ drink.

4

_____ a new law, there are often new crimes. Liquor stores, bars,

5

and restaurants didn't sell alcohol. But some people wanted _____

6

drink. They drank _____ secret, illegal places. When they ordered

7

drinks, they spoke softly. That's why such a place was called a "speakeasy."

It was illegal _____ make alcohol. Liquor companies were closed.

8

But people made alcohol secretly, _____ night. This illegal alcohol

9

was called "moonshine."

It was also illegal _____ sell or carry alcohol. When people sold

10

alcohol, they carried the bottles _____ the leg _____ their

11   12

boot. This crime was called "bootlegging."

The time when it was illegal _____ drink, _____ make, or

13   14

_____ sell alcohol was called Prohibition. _____ Prohibition,

15   16

gangsters controlled the liquor business. They organized the production

_____ "moonshine" and sold it _____ their "speakeasies." It

17   18

was a big business. "Bootlegging" got a new meaning. Gangsters trans-

ported liquor _____ cars, trucks, and ships.

19

Prohibition didn't stop people _____ drinking. But it added new

20

crimes _____ American life. _____ 1933, Prohibition ended.
          21   22

A new law was added _____ the Constitution (the Twenty-first
                        23

Amendment). It canceled the Eighteenth Amendment. This gave Americans

the "freedom" _____ drink. What do you think _____ this
               24   25

freedom?

B. Read the story out loud, whispering the one-syllable prepositions.

Numbers

A. Write the words for the numbers. (These numbers are in the story.)

    1. 18th _____

    2. 21st _____

B. Write the numbers for the words. (These numbers are in the story.)

    1. nineteen thirty-three _____

    2. nineteen twenty _____

Make a Sentence

Choose one subject, one verb, and one object to make a complete sentence.
Four sentences also have expressions of place or time. Write the sentences
on the lines below.

Subject	Verb	Object/Complement	Place/Time
Americans	didn't sell	the Eighteenth	in speakeasies.
Bars	carried	Amendment	in the leg of their
People	controlled	liquor	boot.
People	didn't have	bottles	today.
Gangsters	got	alcohol	during Prohibition.
"Bootlegging"	canceled	the freedom to	
The Twenty-first	have	drink	
Amendment	drank	the illegal liquor	
Americans		business	
		a new meaning	
		the freedom to	
		drink	

1. _____

2. _____

3. _____

4. _____

5. _____

6. _____

7. _____

8. _____

Creative Writing

Use your imagination to write a story about one of the following:

(1) The Day Prohibition Started
(2) The Day Prohibition Ended

_____

_____

_____

_____

_____

_____

_____

_____

_____

_____

_____

_____

_____

_____

_____

_____

_____

_____

Conversation Practice

Discuss these questions with a partner. Then share your answers with the class.

1. Do you think Prohibition was a good idea? Why or why not?
2. Do you think America needs laws about drinking? For example, what should the police do about people who drink and drive?
3. Do you know of any countries where it is illegal to drink? Where? How do the people feel about this policy?
4. What is alcoholism? Name some countries in which alcoholism is a problem. What do these countries do about it?

Chunking

A. Put a slash after each chunk in the story below. The first two sentences are marked for you.
B. Read the story silently. Read in chunks, not word by word.
C. Read the story out loud to the class. Remember, read in chunks.

    The American Constitution guarantees freedom of speech, / religion, / and the press. / In 1920, / a new law / (the Eighteenth Amendment) / was added to the Constitution. / This law said that Americans did not have the freedom to drink.

    With a new law, there are often new crimes. Liquor stores, bars, and restaurants didn't sell alcohol. But some people wanted to drink. They drank in secret, illegal places. When they ordered drinks, they spoke softly. That's why such a place was called a "speakeasy."

It was illegal to make alcohol. Liquor companies were closed. But people made alcohol secretly, at night. This illegal alcohol was called "moonshine."

It was also illegal to sell or carry alcohol. When people sold alcohol, they carried the bottles in the leg of their boot. This crime was called "bootlegging."

The time when it was illegal to drink, to make, or to sell alcohol was called Prohibition. During Prohibition, gangsters controlled the liquor business. They organized the production of "moonshine" and sold it in their "speakeasies." It was a big business. "Bootlegging" got a new meaning. Gangsters transported liquor in cars, trucks, and ships.

Prohibition didn't stop people from drinking. But it added new crimes to American life. In 1933, Prohibition ended. A new law was added to the Constitution (the Twenty-first Amendment). It canceled the Eighteenth Amendment. This gave Americans the "freedom" to drink. What do you think about this freedom?

Vocabulary List

The following words are listed as they appear in the story. The dictionary form is given in parentheses. Read the words out loud. Pay attention to the stress and the number of syllables in each word.

Nouns

Con·sti·tú·tion	cóm·pa·nies		
speech	(company)		
re·lí·gion	móon·shine		
press	bót·tle		
law	leg		
A·ménd·ment	boot		
crime	bóot·leg·ging		
stores (store)	Pro·hi·bí·tion		
bars (bar)	gáng·sters (gangster)		
rés·tau·rants	pro·dúc·tion		
(restaurant)	méan·ing		
ál·co·hol	líq·uor		
drinks (drink)	cars (car)		
spéak·eas·y	trucks (truck)		

Verbs

guar·an·tées	cár·ry
(guarantee)	con·trólled
was ádd·ed	(control)
(add)	ór·gan·ized
said (say)	(organize)
have	trans·pórt·ed
drink	(transport)
sell	stop
ór·dered	ádd·ed (add)
(order)	cán·celed
spoke (speak)	(cancel)
was called	
(call)	

Adjectives

líq·uor	closed (close)
sé·cret	big
il·lé·gal	

Adverbs

sóft·ly	sé·cret·ly
(soft)	(secret)

8

The American Folk Hero

In some countries, the folk hero is the prince. In other countries, it is the soldier or the sailor. In America, the folk hero is the cowboy. He wears a cowboy hat, cowboy boots, and a pair of jeans.

On the one hand, the cowboy is a romantic figure. His life is an adventure. He chases trains and robs banks. He drinks whiskey, fights bandits, and helps women.

On the other hand, the cowboy is a hard worker. His job is dirty and dangerous. He rides a horse and rounds up cattle. He uses a lasso, a branding iron, and a gun. He handles each one masterfully.

The American folk hero didn't come from fairy tales. He came from real life. In the early 1800s, real cowboys moved cattle north to Canada and west to the Pacific Ocean. These cowboys helped win the West.

Buffalo Bill* was one of the most famous cowboys. He was a great rider, buffalo hunter, Indian fighter, and Indian friend. He got the name "Buffalo Bill" because he killed 4,280 buffaloes. What did he do with all that buffalo meat? He distributed it to the people working on the railroad.

Buffalo Bill was also a showman. He organized cowboy shows, or rodeos. He called his group "The Wild West." There were buffalo hunts, shooting contests, and cowboy and Indian fights.

Rodeos made the cowboy popular all over America. Movies made this folk hero famous all over the world.

* William F. Cody (1846–1917).

243 words

Comprehension Questions

A. Write the answer "Yes, he is" or "No, he isn't."

1. Is the cowboy the American folk hero?

   _____

2. Is the cowboy a man with an easy job?

   _____

3. Is Buffalo Bill a famous cowboy?

   _____

4. Is the American cowboy famous all over the world?

   _____

B. Write the answer "Yes, they did" or "No, they didn't."

1. Did cowboys ride horses?

   _____

2. Did cowboys come from fairy tales?

   _____

3. Did cowboys live in the East?

   _____

4. Did cowboys help win the West?

   _____

5. Did rodeos make the cowboy popular?

   _____

C. Write the answer to each question. Use the information given in the story.

1. *Who* killed 4,280 buffaloes?

   _____

2. *Who* are the folk heroes in other countries?

   _____

3. *What* does the cowboy wear?

   _____

4. *What* made the cowboy famous all over the world?

   _____

5. *When* did cowboys move cattle north and west?

   _____

Inference Questions

Answer true or false.

1. Americans like hard work and adventure. _____

2. America built a railroad in the 1800s. _____

3. There are not many movies about cowboys. _____

Skimming

A. Find the *folk heroes* in the story and write them on the lines below. Don't read the story again—just look for the heroes.

_____   _____

_____   _____

B. Find the *animals* in the story.

_____   _____   _____

C. Find the *countries* in the story.

_____   _____

Pronouns

Mark the correct answer for each sentence.

1. Who is "he" in the sentence "He chases trains and robs banks"?

   ( )a. the cowboy
   ( )b. the sailor

2. What is "each one" in the sentence "He handles each one masterfully"?

   ( )a. a horse and cattle
   ( )b. a lasso, a branding iron, and a gun

3. Who is "he" in the sentence "He was a great rider, buffalo hunter, Indian fighter, and Indian friend"?

   ( )a. the American folk hero
   ( )b. Buffalo Bill

Synonyms

Write a synonym for each word below. The synonyms are in the story.

1. children's stories = _____

2. cowboy shows   = _____

3. well-known   = _____

Antonyms

Write an antonym for each word below. The antonyms are in the story.

1. clean   _____

2. safe   _____

3. enemy   _____

Words with More Than One Meaning

Mark the answer that gives the correct meaning of the underlined word in each sentence.

1. In America, the folk hero is the cowboy.
    ( )a. a big sandwich (noun)
    ( )b. a famous, admired person (noun)

2. On the one hand, the cowboy is a romantic figure.
    ( )a. a person as symbol (noun)
    ( )b. shape of the body (noun)

3. He handles each one masterfully.
    ( )a. uses, operates (verb)
    ( )b. parts of tools that are held in the hand (noun)

Vocabulary Practice

Fill in each blank with the correct word.

cowboy	dangerous	Canada
fairy tale	rodeo	lasso
prince	gun	boots
Bill	horse	Pacific
dirty	branding iron	whiskey
bandits		railroad

1. A policeman carries a _____.

2. In Texas, men wear _____ hats.

3. He drinks _____.

4. At the end of the movie, the cowboy killed the _____.

5. It is _____ to walk in the park at night.

6. It isn't easy to ride a _____.

7. "Snow White and the Seven Dwarfs" is a popular _____.

8. _____ is north of the U.S.

9. She always travels by _____.

10. A _____ is made from rope.

11. The name _____ comes from William.

12. A cowboy show is a _____.

13. When it snows, people wear _____ on their feet.

14. When your shoes are _____, you polish them.

15. A _____ puts a mark on cattle to show who the owner is.

16. The largest ocean in the world is the _____ Ocean.

17. A king's son is a _____.

Word Forms

Choose the correct word form for each sentence.

1. *work,*   *worker*
   (verb)   (noun)

   a. They _____ from 9:00 to 5:00.

   b. He is a good _____.

2. *handle*   *hand,*
   (verb)   (noun)

   a. She writes with her left _____.

   b. He knows how to _____ a gun.

3. *rob.*   *robber*
   (verb)   (noun)

   a. He said he didn't _____ the bank.

   b. A _____ took all her money.

4. *live,*   *life*
   (verb)   (noun)

   a. They _____ in Washington, D.C.

   b. She has a hard _____.

5. *ride,*   *rider*
   (verb)   (noun)

   a. He's afraid to _____ a horse.

   b. She's a good _____.

6. *kill*   *killer*
   (verb)   (noun)

   a. The police are looking for the _____.

   b. Did Lee Harvey Oswald _____ President Kennedy?

Prepositions

A. Write the correct preposition in each blank.

from	in	of	on	to	with

_____ some countries, the folk hero is the prince. _____
       1   2
other countries, it is the soldier or the sailor. _____ America, the
                                                                       3
folk hero is the cowboy. He wears a cowboy hat, cowboy boots, and a pair

of jeans.

_____ the one hand, the cowboy is a romantic figure. His life is
       4
an adventure. He chases trains and robs banks. He drinks whiskey, fights

bandits, and helps women.

_____ the other hand, the cowboy is a hard worker. His job is
       5
dirty and dangerous. He rides a horse and rounds up cattle. He uses a lasso,

a branding iron, and a gun. He handles each one masterfully.

The American folk hero didn't come _____ fairy tales. He came
                                                          6
_____ real life. _____ the early 1800s, real cowboys moved
       7   8
cattle north _____ Canada and west _____ the Pacific Ocean.
                    9   10
These cowboys helped win the West.

Buffalo Bill was one _____ the most famous cowboys. He was a
                                    11
great rider, buffalo hunter, Indian fighter, and Indian friend. He got the

name "Buffalo Bill" because he killed 4,280 buffaloes. What did he do

_____ all that buffalo meat? He distributed it _____ the
       12   13
people working _____ the railroad.
                          14
Buffalo Bill was also a showman. He organized cowboy shows, or rodeos.

He called his group "The Wild West." There were buffalo hunts, shooting contests, and cowboy and Indian fights.

Rodeos made the cowboy popular all over America. Movies made this folk hero famous all over the world.

B. Read the story out loud, whispering the prepositions. (They are all one-syllable prepositions.)

Numbers

Write the numbers for the words. (These numbers are in the story.)

1. the eighteen hundreds _____

2. four thousand, two hundred eighty _____

Make a Sentence

Choose one subject, one verb, and one object to make a complete sentence. Write the sentences on the lines below.

Subject	Verb	Object/Complement
The cowboy	is	a romantic figure.
His life	uses	trains.
He	came from	a lasso and a gun.
The cowboy	was	real life.
The American folk hero	is	the West.
Real cowboys	killed	a famous cowboy.
Buffalo Bill	organized	an adventure.
He	chases	4,280 buffaloes.
Buffalo Bill	helped win	rodeos.

1. _____

2. _____

3. _____

4. _____

5. _____

6. _____

7. _____

8. _____

9. _____

Creative Writing

Write a story about one of the following:

        (1) William F. Cody
        (2) The Best Cowboy Movie
        (3) A Rodeo

_____

_____

_____

_____

_____

_____

_____

_____

_____

_____

_____

_____

_____

_____

_____

_____

_____

_____

Conversation Practice

Discuss these questions with a partner. Then share your answers with the class.

1. Why is the cowboy so popular?
2. Who is the most popular folk hero in your country?
3. Does America need cowboys today?
4. Each generation has different heroes. Who are the heroes of your generation? Who are the heroes of your parents' generation?

Chunking

A. Put a slash after each chunk in the story below. The first two sentences are marked for you.
B. Read the story silently. Read in chunks, not word by word.
C. Read the story out loud to the class. Remember, read in chunks.

In some countries,   /   the folk hero is the prince.   /   In other countries,   /   it is the soldier or the sailor.   /   In America, the folk hero is the cowboy. He wears a cowboy hat, cowboy boots, and a pair of jeans.

On the one hand, the cowboy is a romantic figure. His life is an adventure. He chases trains and robs banks. He drinks whiskey, fights bandits, and helps women.

On the other hand, the cowboy is a hard worker. His job is dirty and dangerous. He rides a horse and rounds up cattle. He uses a lasso, a branding iron, and a gun. He handles each one masterfully.

The American folk hero didn't come from fairy tales. He came from real life. In the early 1800s, real cowboys moved cattle north to Canada and west to the Pacific Ocean. These cowboys helped win the West.

Buffalo Bill was one of the most famous cowboys. He was a great rider, buffalo hunter, Indian fighter, and Indian friend. He got the name "Buffalo Bill" because he killed 4,280 buffaloes. What did he do with all that buffalo meat? He distributed it to the people working on the railroad.

Buffalo Bill was also a showman. He organized cowboy shows, or rodeos. He called his group "The Wild West." There were buffalo hunts, shooting contests, and cowboy and Indian fights.

Rodeos made the cowboy popular all over America. Movies made this folk hero famous all over the world.

Vocabulary List

The following words are listed as they appear in the story. The dictionary form is given in parentheses. Read the words out loud. Pay attention to the stress and the number of syllables in each word.

Adjectives		*Nouns*	*Verbs*
folk	hé·ro	í·ron	wears (wear)
ców·boy	prince	gun	chás·es (chase)
ro·mán·tic	sól·dier	tales (tale)	robs (rob)
hard	sáil·or	Cán·a·da	drinks (drink)
dírt·y	ców·boy	Ó·cean	fights (fight)
dán·ger·ous	hat	West	helps (help)
bránd·ing	boots (boot)	Bill	rides (ride)
(brand)	pair	ríd·er	rounds up (round)
fáir·y	jeans (jean)	búf·fa·lo	hán·dles (handle)
real	hand	húnt·er	come from (come)
Pa·cíf·ic	fíg·ure	fíght·er	moved (move)
great	ad·vén·ture	friend	killed (kill)
Ín·di·an	trains (train)	meat	do
búf·fa·lo	banks (bank)	ráil·road	dis·tríb·ut·ed
Wild	whís·key	shów·man	(distribute)
shóot·ing	bán·dits (bandit)	shows (show)	ór·gan·ized
(shoot)	wóm·en (woman)	ró·de·os (rodeo)	(organize)
	wórk·er	group	called (call)
	job	hunts (hunt)	
	horse	cón·tests (contest)	
	cát·tle	fights (fight)	
	lás·so	móv·ies (movie)	

Adverbs

más·ter·ful·ly
(masterful)
north
west
ál·so

9

Fall Back, Spring Ahead

Two times a year, clocks are changed in America. It's a law. On the last Sunday in April, clocks are moved ahead one hour. This is called Daylight Saving Time. On the last Sunday in October, clocks are moved back one hour to Standard Time. It's very simple, but many people can't remember to change their clocks. Maybe that's because they don't know the story behind it.

It all started back in 1784. Benjamin Franklin, an American writer, diplomat, and inventor, suggested Daylight Saving Time in an essay. People thought he was joking.

Many years later, during World War I and World War II, people realized that Benjamin Franklin was right. The country needed energy. It was necessary to save electricity, but how? One way was to change the time. In the spring and summer, the sun rises earlier. To take advantage of this early sunlight, clocks were moved ahead one hour. So now, people who usually woke up at 8:00 really woke up at 7:00. If they normally turned on the lights at 5:00 in the evening, now they turned on the lights at 6:00. They had an extra hour of daylight, so they used less electricity.

During the wars, changing the clocks was just an experiment. Daylight Saving Time didn't become a law until 1966. But this didn't make it any easier to remember. People still asked each other, "When do you change the time, and which way?" To make it a little easier, Americans just say, "Fall back, spring ahead."

253 words

Comprehension Questions

A. Write the answer, using the underlined word.

Example: Is Daylight Saving Time a law in the United States?

> *Yes, it is.*

1. Are clocks moved back on the last Sunday in October?

2. Are clocks changed three times a year in America?

3. Were clocks changed during World War I and World War II?

4. Does Daylight Saving Time save electricity?

5. Do Americans say, "Fall ahead, spring back"?

B. Write the answer to each question. Use the information given in the story.

1. *When* are clocks moved ahead in America?

2. *When* are clocks moved back in America?

3. *When* did Benjamin Franklin suggest Daylight Saving Time?

4. *When* did Daylight Saving Time become a law?

5. *What* do we call the time from the last Sunday in October to the last Sunday in April?

_____

6. *What* do we call the time from the last Sunday in April to the last Sunday in October?

_____

7. *Why* were clocks changed in America during World War I and II?

_____

8. *Who* suggested Daylight Saving Time in an essay?

_____

Inference Questions

Answer true or false.

1. Changing the time saved electricity during the war. _____

2. If you say, "Fall back, spring ahead," you will always remember to change your clocks. _____

3. The U.S. government thinks Daylight Saving Time is a good idea.

_____

Skimming

A. Find the *months* in the story and write them on the lines below. Don't read the story again—just look for the months.

_____   _____

B. Find the *years* in the story.

_____   _____

C. Find the *seasons* in the story.

_____   _____

Pronouns

Mark the correct answer for each sentence.

1. What is "it" in the sentence "It's a law"?

   ( )a. Standard Time
   ( )b. changing the clocks

2. What is "this" in the sentence "This is called Daylight Saving Time"?

   ( )a. moving the clocks ahead
   ( )b. moving the clocks back

3. Who is "he" in the sentence "People thought he was joking"?

   ( )a. the President
   ( )b. Benjamin Franklin

Synonyms

Write a synonym for each word below. The synonyms are in the story.

1. forward   = _____

2. began   = _____

3. proposed = _____

4. normally = _____

Antonyms

Write an antonym for each word below. The antonyms are in the story.

1. first   _____

2. forget   _____

3. serious   _____

4. unnecessary _____

5. use   _____

6. later   _____

7. more   _____

Words with More Than One Meaning

Mark the answer that gives the correct meaning of the underlined word in each sentence.

1. It's very simple, but many people can't remember to <u>change</u> their clocks.

   (x)a. coins, money (noun)
   ( )b. move (verb)

2. Maybe that's because they don't know the <u>story</u> behind it.

   (x)a. history, information (noun)
   ( )b. floor of a building (noun)

3. The <u>country</u> needed energy.

   (x)a. nation (noun)
   ( )b. land outside the city (noun)

Vocabulary Practice

Fill in each blank with the correct word.

simple	energy	started	story
essay	law	fall	electricity
spring	experiment	clock	suggested

1. Your _____ is wrong. It's exactly 5:30.

2. You can't drive over 55 miles an hour. It's a _____.

3. The exam was so _____, he got 100 percent.

4. The ballet _____ at 8:00 and ended at 10:00.

5. Another word for autumn is _____.

6. Electricity and oil are two kinds of _____.

7. The rabbits died during the _____.

8. We wrote an _____ for homework.

9. Tony _____ that we eat in a Chinese restaurant.

10. Every night, he reads a _____ to his children.

11. _____ begins on March 20 or 21 in the U.S.

12. She works at home, so she uses a lot of _____.

Word Forms

Choose the correct word form for each sentence.

1. *change*   *change*
   (verb)   (noun)

   a. Fashions _____ every year.

   b. He's not happy at his job. He needs a _____.

2. *year*   *yearly*
   (noun)   (adjective)

   a. In what _____ were you born?

   b. She's going to the dentist for her _____ check-up.

3. *remember*   *memory*
   (verb)   (noun)

   a. He has a good _____ for names.

   b. Do you _____ your first day of school?

4. *need*   *necessity*   *necessary*
   (verb)   (noun)   (adjective)

   a. Many countries _____ food.

   b. A dishwasher isn't a _____.

   c. It's _____ to leave a tip in a restaurant in the U.S.

Prepositions

A. Write the correct preposition in each blank.

at	behind	during	in	of	on	to	until

Two times a year, clocks are changed _____ America. It's a law.

_____ the last Sunday in April, clocks are moved ahead one hour.
2

This is called Daylight Saving Time. _____ the last Sunday in
3

October, clocks are moved back one hour _____ Standard Time. It's
4

very simple, but many people can't remember _____ change their
5

clocks. Maybe that's because they don't know the story _____ it.
6

It all started back _____ 1784. Benjamin Franklin, an American
7

writer, diplomat, and inventor, suggested Daylight Saving Time _____
8

an essay. People thought he was joking.

Many years later, _____ World War I and World War II, people
9

realized that Benjamin Franklin was right. The country needed energy. It

was necessary _____ save electricity, but how? One way was
10

_____ change the time. _____ the spring and summer, the
11$$12

sun rises earlier. _____ take advantage _____ this early
13$$14

sunlight, clocks were moved ahead one hour. So now, people who usually

woke up _____ 8:00 really woke up _____ 7:00. If they nor-
15$$16

mally turned on the lights _____ 5:00 _____ the evening,
$17$18

now they turned on the lights _____ 6:00. They had an extra hour
19

_____ daylight, so they used less electricity.
20

_____ the wars, changing the clocks was just an experiment.
        21

Daylight Saving Time didn't become a law _____ 1966. But this
                                                22

didn't make it any easier _____ remember. People still asked each
                                23

other, "When do you change the time, and which way?" _____ make
                                                            24

it a little easier, Americans just say, "Fall back, spring ahead."

B. Read the story out loud, whispering the one-syllable prepositions.

Numbers

Write the numbers for the words. (These numbers are in the story.)

  1. seventeen eighty-four_____

  2. nineteen sixty-six   _____

Make a Sentence

Choose one subject, one verb, and one object to make a complete sentence.
Write the sentences on the lines below.

Subject	Verb	Object/Complement
Many people	say	Daylight Saving Time.
Benjamin Franklin	became	their clocks.
	can't remember	energy.
The country	to change	an extra hour of daylight.
Changing the clocks	needed	less electricity.
	used	a law.
People	suggested	"Fall back, spring ahead."
They	was	an experiment.
Daylight Saving Time	had	
Americans		

1. _____

2. _____

3. _____

4. _____

5. _____

6. _____

7. _____

8. _____

Sentence Scramble

Put the words in the correct order to make a sentence. Write your sentences on the lines below.

1. usually   spring   Americans   the   like

   _____

2. remember   summer   he   when   can't   starts   the

   _____

3. wrote   time   essay   she   an   about

   _____

4. Sunday   story   war   the   us   told   a   about   he

   last

   _____

Conversation Practice

Discuss these questions with a partner. Then share your answers with the class.

1. Do you think Daylight Saving Time is a good idea? Why or why not?
2. What are some other ways a country can save energy?

3. The United States has four time zones. In other words, there are four parts of the country with different times. (See the map below.) The time zones are called Eastern Standard Time; Central Standard Time; Mountain Standard Time; and Pacific Standard Time. What are some of the problems people can have because there is more than one time zone?

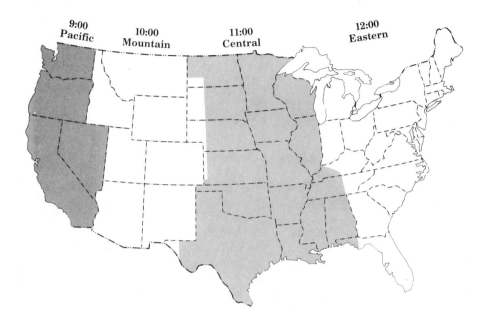

Chunking

A. Put a slash after each chunk in the story below. The first two sentences are marked for you.
B. Read the story silently. Read in chunks, not word by word.
C. Read the story out loud to the class. Remember, read in chunks.

Two times a year, / clocks are changed in America. / It's a law. / On the last Sunday in April, clocks are moved ahead one hour. This is called Daylight Saving Time. On the last Sunday in October, clocks are moved back one hour to Standard Time. It's very simple, but many people can't remember to change their clocks. Maybe that's because they don't know the story behind it.

It all started back in 1784. Benjamin Franklin, an American writer, diplomat, and inventor, suggested Daylight Saving Time in an essay. People thought he was joking.

Many years later, during World War I and World War II, people realized that Benjamin Franklin was right. The country needed energy. It was necessary to save electricity, but how? One way was to change the time. In the spring and summer, the sun rises earlier. To take advantage of this early sunlight, clocks were moved ahead one hour. So now, people who usually woke up at 8:00 really woke up at 7:00. If they normally turned on the lights at 5:00 in the evening, now they turned on the lights at 6:00. They had an extra hour of daylight, so they used less electricity.

During the wars, changing the clocks was just an experiment. Daylight Saving Time didn't become a law until 1966. But this didn't make it any easier to remember. People still asked each other, "When do you change the time, and which way?" To make it a little easier, Americans just say, "Fall back, spring ahead."

Vocabulary List

The following words are listed as they appear in the story. The dictionary form is given in parentheses. Read the words out loud. Pay attention to the stress and the number of syllables in each word.

Adjectives	*Nouns*	*Verbs*	*Adverbs*
dáy·light	year	moved (move)	a·héad
sáv·ing (save)	clocks (clock)	re·mém·ber	back
last	Sún·day	change	eár·li·er
stán·dard	Á·pril	know	(early)
sím·ple	hour	sug·gést·ed (suggest)	ú·su·al·ly
má·ny	dáy·light	was jók·ing (joke)	réal·ly
néc·es·sar·y	Oc·tó·ber	néed·ed (need)	nór·mal·ly
éx·tra	stór·y	save	
less	Bén·ja·min	rís·es (rise)	
just	Fránk·lin	woke up (wake)	
éa·si·er (easy)	és·say	turned (turn)	
lít·tle	én·er·gy	be·cóme	
	e·lec·tríc·i·ty	asked (ask)	
	súm·mer		
	ad·ván·tage		
	sún·light		
	lights (light)		
	éve·ning		
	ex·pér·i·ment		
	fall		
	spring		

10

This Land Is Your Land

Woody Guthrie was a singer and a songwriter. He was born in 1912 in a small town in Oklahoma. Life wasn't easy when he was a boy. His house burned down. His sister died in an accident. His mother went to a mental institution. At fifteen, Woody didn't have a family anymore.

He was on his own. He sold newspapers. He shined shoes. He picked grapes and drilled for oil. He painted signs and washed dishes. He traveled across the country by train. His baggage was a guitar and a harmonica. He was a twentieth-century traveling minstrel. He sang at parties, at rodeos, in bars, and at home. "Home" was usually a friend's apartment, a cheap hotel, or the back seat of a car.

The little guy with the guitar sang hobo songs and work songs:

> *You get a hammer and I'll get a nail,*
> *You catch a bird and I'll catch a snail,*
> *You bring a board and I'll bring a saw,*
> *And we'll build a house for the baby-o.*©

He sang peace songs and war songs, too:

> *I didn't boil myself no coffee,*
> *I didn't boil no tea,*
> *I made a run for that recruitin' office—*
> *Uncle Sam, make room for me!*©

Woody Guthrie couldn't read music, but he wrote more than one thousand songs. Many of them became American classics. They were about working people, poor people, hungry people. But they were happy songs, optimistic songs. "I hate a song that makes you think that you're not any good," Woody said.

Woody Guthrie, the folk singer, was becoming popular. His music was on the radio. A record company recorded his songs. In 1940, his first album came out. Businessmen wanted to control him. They told him what to do. But Woody didn't listen, and, once again, he was on the road.

Woody Guthrie didn't want money. He didn't want fame. He was a true son of his country. He wanted to be free.

This land is your land, this land is my land
From California to the New York island.
From the redwood forest to the Gulf Stream waters
This land was made for you and me.©

361 words

Comprehension Questions

A. Write the answer "Yes, he did" or "No, he didn't."

1. Did Woody Guthrie write songs?

   _____

2. Did he live in a small town when he was a boy?

   _____

3. Did he have an easy life when he was a boy?

   _____

4. Did he shine shoes?

   _____

5. Did he write songs about poor people?

   _____

6. Did he sing only work songs?

   _____

7. Did he become a businessman?

   _____

8. Did he want money and fame?

   _____

B. Write the answer to each question. Use the information given in the story.

1. *Where* did Woody Guthrie live when he was a boy?

   _____

2. *How* did his sister die?

   _____

3. *How* did he travel across the country?

_____

4. *What* did he carry when he traveled?

_____

5. *How many* songs did he write?

_____

6. *When* did his first album come out?

_____

7. *What* did Woody Guthrie want?

_____

Inference Questions

Answer true or false.

1. Woody Guthrie was one of the greatest songwriters of the twentieth

   century. _____

2. Woody Guthrie was an independent person. _____

3. Woody Guthrie was a rich man. _____

4. Music was very important to Woody Guthrie. _____

Skimming

A. Find the *jobs* in the story and write them on the lines below. Don't read
   the story again—just look for the jobs.

   *selling newspapers*_____   _____

   _____   _____

_____   _____

_____   _____

B. Find the different kinds of *songs* in the story.

hobo songs _____   _____

_____   _____

C. Find the *places* where Woody sang.

at parties _____   _____

_____   _____

Pronouns

Mark the correct answer for each sentence.

1. Who is "he" in the sentence "He was born in a small town in Oklahoma"?

   (✗)a. Woody Guthrie
   ( )b. Woody Guthrie's father

2. What are "they" in the sentence "They were about working people, poor people, hungry people"?

   ( )a. peace songs
   (✗)b. Woody Guthrie's songs

3. Who are "they" in the sentence "They told him what to do"?

   ( )a. folk singers
   (✗)b. businessmen

Synonyms

Write a synonym for each word below. The synonyms are in the story.

1. little   = _____

2. simple   = _____

3. inexpensive = _____

4. positive   = _____

5. album   = _____

Antonyms

Write an antonym for each word below. The antonyms are in the story.

1. bought   _____

2. front   _____

3. war   _____

4. rich   _____

5. sad   _____

6. bad   _____

7. last   _____

Words with More Than One Meaning

Mark the answer that gives the correct meaning of the underlined word in each sentence.

1. He sang at parties, at rodeos, in bars, and at home.

   ( )a. political organizations (noun)
   (✓)b. social gatherings (noun)

2. In 1940, his first album came out.

   (✓)a. long-playing record (noun)
   ( )b. book for photographs (noun)

3. He wanted to be free.

   (✓)a. independent (adjective)
   ( )b. without cost (adjective) hình dung từ.

Vocabulary Practice

Fill in each blank with the correct word.

album	burned	record
accident	dishes	baggage
train	minstrels	cheap
guitar	fame	shined
war	town	peace
radio	poor	classics
free	folk	businessman
optimistic	picked	back
mental		

1. She doesn't want to live in a small _____ town _____.

2. His psychiatrist wants to put him in a _____ institution.

3. There was a fire and the whole building _____ burned _____ down.

4. Their son died in a car _____ accident _____.

5. Before he went to work, he _____ shined _____ his shoes.

6. She _____ picked _____ grapes in California.

7. Her husband always washes the _____ dishes _____.

8. It's faster to travel by _____ train _____ than by bus.

9. When you get off a plane, you must pick up your _____ baggage _____.

10. A _____ has six or twelve strings.

11. In the Middle Ages, _____ played music for people.

12. A room in that hotel costs $100 a night. That isn't _____ free _____!

13. The children don't like to sit in the _____ back _____ seat of the car.

14. Do you think there will be a _____ peace _____ between the United States and the Soviet Union?

15. The leaders of both countries say they want _____.

16. "This Land Is Your Land" and other Guthrie songs are American

_____.

17. They have almost no money. They are very _____.

18. She always says everything will be okay. She's very _____.

19. Peter, Paul, and Mary were popular _____ singers in the 1960s.

20. They listen to the _____ all day.

21. She is the president of a big _____ company.

22. He loves music, so he buys at least one new _____ every week.

23. He is studying economics because he wants to be a _____.

24. She doesn't want _____. She wants a quiet life.

25. Many people come to America because they want to be _____.

Word Forms

Choose the correct word form for each sentence.

1. *sing*   *singer*   *song*
   (verb)   (noun)   (noun)

   a. She is an opera _____.

   b. He wrote a new _____.

   c. Do you _____ in the shower?

2. *die*   *death*
   (verb)   (noun)

   a. Most people are afraid to _____.

   b. He had a painful _____.

3. *shine*   *shiny*
   (verb)   (adjective)

   a. Your furniture is very _____shiny_____.

   b. She hates to _____shine_____ her shoes.

4. *paint*   *painter*   *paint*
   (verb)   (noun)   (noun)

   a. When did you _____paint_____ your
   apartment?

   b. What color _____paint_____ did you buy?

   c. He is a house _____painter_____.

5. *sit*   *seat*
   (verb) (noun)

   a. This is a comfortable _____.

   b. Please _____ down, everyone.

6. *peace*   *peaceful*
   (noun)   (adjective)

   a. This is a _____ place.

   b. After the war, there were many years of _____peace_____.

7. *music*   *musician*
   (noun)   (noun)

   a. He likes rock _____music_____.

   b. She is a jazz _____.

8. *classics*   *classical*
   (noun)   (adjective)

   a. He listens to _____classical_____ music.

   b. Shakespeare's plays are _____ of English litera-
   ture.

9. *recórd*   *récord*   *récord*
   (verb)   (noun)   (adjective)

   a. Did you ever _____ your voice?

   b. She has every _____ that group ever made.

   c. He works in the _____ business.

Prepositions

A. Write the correct preposition in each blank.

about   across   at   by   for   in   of   on   to   with

Woody Guthrie was a singer and a songwriter. He was born _____
                                                          1

1912 _____ a small town _____ Oklahoma. Life wasn't easy
           2   3

when he was a boy. His house burned down. His sister died _____
                                                              4

an accident. His mother went _____ a mental institution. _____
                                 5   6

fifteen, Woody didn't have a family anymore.

He was _____ his own. He sold newspapers. He shined shoes. He
           7

picked grapes and drilled _____ oil. He painted signs and washed
                               8

dishes. He traveled ___across___ the country _____ train. His bag-
                         9   10

gage was a guitar and a harmonica. He was a twentieth-century traveling

minstrel. He sang _____ parties, _____ rodeos, _____
                       11   12   13

bars, and _____ home. "Home" was usually a friend's apartment, a
               14

cheap hotel, or the back seat _____ a car.
                                   15

The little guy _____ the guitar sang hobo songs and work songs:
                   16

You get a hammer and I'll get a nail,
You catch a bird and I'll catch a snail,
You bring a board and I'll bring a saw,
And we'll build a house for the baby-o.©

He sang peace songs and war songs, too:

I didn't boil myself no coffee,
I didn't boil no tea,
I made a run for that recruitin' office—
Uncle Sam, make room for me!©

Woody Guthrie couldn't read music, but he wrote more than one thousand songs. Many _____ them became American classics. They were
                        17
_____ working people, poor people, hungry people. But they were
       18
happy songs, optimistic songs. "I hate a song that makes you think that you're not any good," Woody said.

Woody Guthrie, the folk singer, was becoming popular. His music was

_____ the radio. A record company recorded his songs. _____
       19   20
1940, his first album came out. Businessmen wanted _____ control
                                                                  21
him. They told him what _____ do. But Woody didn't listen, and,
                              22
once again, he was _____ the road.
                        23
Woody Guthrie didn't want money. He didn't want fame. He was a true

son _____ his country. He wanted _____ be free.
        24   25

This land is your land, this land is my land
From California to the New York island.
From the redwood forest to the Gulf Stream waters
This land was made for you and me.©

B. Read the story out loud, whispering the one-syllable prepositions.

Numbers

A. Write the words for the numbers. (These numbers are in the story.)

1. 1,000 _____

2. 15 _____

3. 20th _____

B. Write the numbers for the words. (These numbers are in the story.)

1. nineteen twelve _____

2. nineteen forty _____

Make a Sentence

Choose one subject, one verb, and one object to make a complete sentence. Write the sentences on the lines below.

Subject	Verb	Object/Complement
Woody Guthrie	sold	a friend's apartment.
He	became	his songs.
He	shined	a singer and a songwriter.
"Home"	was	music.
The little guy	wanted to be	shoes.
with the guitar	was	American classics.
He	didn't want	hobo songs and work songs.
Many of his songs	recorded	free.
They	couldn't	newspapers.
A record company	read	money or fame.
Woody Guthrie	were	optimistic songs.
He	sang	

1. _____

2. _____

3. _____

4. _____

5. _____

6. _____

7. _____

8. _____

9. _____

10. _____

11. _____

Creative Writing

Write a story about one of the following:

      1. John Lennon of the Beatles
      2. Arlo Guthrie, Woody Guthrie's son
      3. A famous singer from your native country

_____

_____

_____

_____

_____

_____

_____

_____

_____

_____

_____

_____

_____

_____

_____

_____

_____

_____

_____

_____

Conversation Practice

Discuss these questions with a partner. Then share your answers with the class.

1. What kinds of songs do you like? Why?
2. Who is your favorite singer?
3. Which American singers are popular in your native country? Why do people like them?
4. Is it possible for a singer to be free and independent, like Woody Guthrie, today?

Chunking

A. Put a slash after each chunk in the story below. The first two sentences are marked for you.
B. Read the story silently. Read in chunks, not word by word.
C. Read the story out loud to the class. Remember, read in chunks.

   Woody Guthrie   /   was a singer and a songwriter.   /   He was born in 1912   /   in a small town in Oklahoma. Life wasn't easy when he was a boy. His house burned down. His sister died in an accident. His mother went to a mental institution. At fifteen, Woody didn't have a family anymore.

He was on his own. He sold newspapers. He shined shoes. He picked grapes and drilled for oil. He painted signs and washed dishes. He traveled across the country by train. His baggage was a guitar and a harmonica. He was a twentieth-century traveling minstrel. He sang at parties, at rodeos, in bars, and at home. "Home" was usually a friend's apartment, a cheap hotel, or the back seat of a car.

The little guy with the guitar sang hobo songs and work songs:

> *You get a hammer and I'll get a nail,*
> *You catch a bird and I'll catch a snail,*
> *You bring a board and I'll bring a saw,*
> *And we'll build a house for the baby-o.*©

He sang peace songs and war songs, too:

> *I didn't boil myself no coffee,*
> *I didn't boil no tea,*
> *I made a run for that recruitin' office—*
> *Uncle Sam, make room for me!*©

Woody Guthrie couldn't read music, but he wrote more than one thousand songs. Many of them became American classics. They were about working people, poor people, hungry people. But they were happy songs, optimistic songs. "I hate a song that makes you think that you're not any good," Woody said.

Woody Guthrie, the folk singer, was becoming popular. His music was on the radio. A record company recorded his songs. In 1940, his first album came out. Businessmen wanted to control him. They told him what to do. But Woody didn't listen, and, once again, he was on the road.

Woody Guthrie didn't want money. He didn't want fame. He was a true son of his country. He wanted to be free.

> *This land is your land, this land is my land*
> *From California to the New York island.*
> *From the redwood forest to the Gulf Stream waters*
> *This land was made for you and me.*©

Vocabulary List

The following words are listed as they appear in the story. The dictionary form is given in parentheses. Read the words out loud. Pay attention to the stress and the number of syllables in each word.

Adjectives	*Nouns*		*Verbs*
small	Wóod·y	mín·strel	died (die)
éas·y	Gúth·rie	pár·ties (party)	shined (shine)
mén·tal	síng·er	home	picked (pick)
tráv·el·ing	sóng·writ·er	friend	washed (wash)
(travel)	town	a·párt·ment	tráv·eled (travel)
cheap	O·kla·hó·ma	ho·tél	read
back	boy	seat	hate
hó·bo	sís·ter	car	makes (make)
work	ác·ci·dent	guy	think
peace	móth·er	songs (song)	was be·cóm·ing
war	in·sti·tú·tion	mú·sic	(become)
wórk·ing (work)	fám·ily	clás·sics (classic)	re·córd·ed (record)
hún·gry	shoes (shoe)	rá·di·o	came out (come)
háp·py	grapes	cóm·pa·ny	con·tról
op·ti·mís·tic	(grape)	ál·bum	told (tell)
folk	signs (sign)	búsi·ness·men	lís·ten
réc·ord	dísh·es	(businessman)	
first	(dish)	road	
true	train	món·ey	
free	bág·gage	fame	
	gui·tár	son	
	har·món·i·ca		

Appendix 1

Numbers

Cardinal Numbers

1	one
2	two
3	three
4	four
5	five
6	six
7	seven
8	eight
9	nine
10	ten
11	eleven
12	twelve
13	thirteen
14	fourteen
15	fifteen
16	sixteen
17	seventeen
18	eighteen
19	nineteen
20	twenty
21	twenty-one

Ordinal Numbers

1st	first
2nd	second
3rd	third
4th	fourth
5th	fifth
6th	sixth
7th	seventh
8th	eighth
9th	ninth
10th	tenth
11th	eleventh
12th	twelfth
13th	thirteenth
14th	fourteenth
15th	fifteenth
16th	sixteenth
17th	seventeenth
18th	eighteenth
19th	nineteenth
20th	twentieth
21st	twenty-first

Cardinal Numbers

30	thirty
40	forty
50	fifty
60	sixty
70	seventy
80	eighty
90	ninety
100	one hundred
1,000	one thousand
100,000	one hundred thousand
1,000,000	one million

Ordinal Numbers

30th	thirtieth
40th	fortieth
50th	fiftieth
60th	sixtieth
70th	seventieth
80th	eightieth
90th	ninetieth
100th	one hundredth
1,000th	one thousandth
100,000th	one hundred thousandth
1,000,000th	one millionth

Regular and Irregular Verbs

Simple Infinitive (dictionary form)	Past Tense	Past Participle
add	added	added
admire	admired	admired
arrive	arrived	arrived
ask	asked	asked
*bear	bore	born
*become	became	become
*begin	began	begun
believe	believed	believed
*build	built	built
burn	burned	burned
call	called	called
cancel	canceled	canceled
carry	carried	carried
change	changed	changed
chase	chased	chased
*come	came	come
control	controlled	controlled
design	designed	designed
destroy	destroyed	destroyed
die	died	died

*Irregular Verbs

Simple Infinitive (dictionary form)	Past Tense	Past Participle
discover	discovered	discovered
distribute	distributed	distributed
*do	did	done
drill	drilled	drilled
*drink	drank	drunk
*eat	ate	eaten
end	ended	ended
*fight	fought	fought
*get	got	gotten
*give	gave	given
*grow	grew	grown
guarantee	guaranteed	guaranteed
handle	handled	handled
hate	hated	hated
*have	had	had
help	helped	helped
*hold	held	held
immigrate	immigrated	immigrated
import	imported	imported
joke	joked	joked
kill	killed	killed
*know	knew	known
lift	lifted	lifted
like	liked	liked
listen	listened	listened
live	lived	lived
look	looked	looked
*lose	lost	lost
love	loved	loved
*make	made	made
*mean	meant	meant
move	moved	moved
name	named	named
need	needed	needed

Simple Infinitive (dictionary form)	Past Tense	Past Participle
order	ordered	ordered
organize	organized	organized
paint	painted	painted
pick	picked	picked
point	pointed	pointed
*read	read	read
*rebuild	rebuilt	rebuilt
record	recorded	recorded
remember	remembered	remembered
represent	represented	represented
*ride	rode	ridden
*rise	rose	risen
round (up)	rounded (up)	rounded (up)
save	saved	saved
*say	said	said
*see	saw	seen
*sell	sold	sold
*shine	shone	shone
*speak	spoke	spoken
*stand	stood	stood
start	started	started
stop	stopped	stopped
suggest	suggested	suggested
*tell	told	told
*think	thought	thought
transport	transported	transported
travel	traveled	traveled
turn	turned	turned
use	used	used
*wake (up)	woke (up)	woken (up)
want	wanted	wanted
wash	washed	washed
*wear	wore	worn
welcome	welcomed	welcomed
*win	won	won
*write	wrote	written

Appendix 2

Some Facts About the United States of America

Form of government: a federal republic.

Official language: English.

Official religion: none.

Population: 226,545,805 (1980 census).

Capital: Washington, D.C.

Monetary unit: 1 dollar = 100 cents.

Race: (1980 census): 83.2% white
                      11.7% black
                        .6% American Indian, Eskimo, and Aleut
                     1.5% Asian and Pacific Islander
                     3.0% Other

Life expectancy at birth: 73.3 years.

The seasons: Winter begins December 22 or 23.
                Spring begins March 20 or 21.
                Summer begins June 21 or 22.
                Fall begins September 22 or 23.

THE LARGEST . . . THE SMALLEST . . . THE HIGHEST . . . THE
LONGEST . . . THE FIRST

The largest state is Alaska—570,833 square miles, 1,478,458 sq. km.

The smallest state is Rhode Island—1,055 sq. mi., 2,732 sq. km.

The largest population is in California—23,667,902 (1980 census).

The smallest population is in Alaska—401,851 (1980 census).

The highest mountain is Mount McKinley (named after President William
McKinley) in Alaska—20,320 feet high.

The longest river is the Mississippi River—2,470 miles long.

The first English settlement was Jamestown, Virginia (1607).

Each state has a special name. Some of these names are:

> The Sunshine State (Florida)
> The Show Me State (Missouri)
> The Garden State (New Jersey)
> The Lone Star State (Texas)
> The Green Mountain State (Vermont)
> The Empire State (New York)

Federal Legal Holidays in the United States

New Years Day—January 1
Washington's Birthday—third Monday in February
    (Traditional Washington's Birthday—February 22)
Memorial Day—last Monday in May
Independence Day—July 4
Labor Day—first Monday in September
Columbus Day—second Monday in October
Veterans Day—November 11
Thanksgiving Day—fourth Thursday in November
Christmas Day—December 25

The National Anthem: *The Star-Spangled Banner*

Written by Francis Scott Key during the War of 1812.

O say, can you see by the dawn's early light,
    What so proudly we hailed at the twilight's last gleaming?
Whose broad stripes and bright stars through the perilous fight,
    O'er the ramparts we watched, were so gallantly streaming!
        And the rocket's red glare,
        The bombs bursting in air
Gave proof through the night that our flag was still there;
    O say, does that star spangled banner yet wave
    O'er the land of the free and the home of the brave?

American Presidents

Name	*Term of Office*
1. George Washington	1789–1797
2. John Adams	1797–1801
3. Thomas Jefferson	1801–1809
4. James Madison	1809–1817
5. James Monroe	1817–1825
6. John Quincy Adams	1825–1829
7. Andrew Jackson	1829–1837
8. Martin Van Buren	1837–1841
9. William Henry Harrison	3/4/41–4/4/41
10. John Tyler	1841–1845
11. James K. Polk	1845–1849
12. Zachary Taylor	1849–7/9/50
13. Millard Fillmore	1850–1853
14. Franklin Pierce	1853–1857
15. James Buchanan	1857–1861
16. Abraham Lincoln	1861–4/14/65
17. Andrew Johnson	1865–1869
18. Ulysses S. Grant	1869–1877
19. Rutherford B. Hayes	1877–1881
20. James A. Garfield	3/4/81–9/19/81
21. Chester A. Arthur	1881–1885
22. Grover Cleveland	1885–1889 and 1893–1897
23. Benjamin Harrison	1889–1893
24. William McKinley	1897–9/14/01
25. Theodore Roosevelt	1901–1909
26. William Howard Taft	1909–1913
27. Woodrow Wilson	1913–1921
28. Warren G. Harding	1921–8/2/23
29. Calvin Coolidge	1923–1929
30. Herbert Hoover	1929–1933
31. Franklin D. Roosevelt	1933–4/12/45
32. Harry S. Truman	1945–1953
33. Dwight D. Eisenhower	1953–1961
34. John F. Kennedy	1961–11/22/63
35. Lyndon B. Johnson	1963–1969
36. Richard M. Nixon	1969–1974
37. Gerald R. Ford	1974–1977
38. Jimmy Carter	1977–1981
39. Ronald Reagan	1981–

A Map of the United States of America

Answer Key

1. The Discovery of America

Comprehension Questions

A. 1. true
2. false
3. true
4. true
5. false
6. false
7. true
8. true
9. true

B. 1. No, he didn't.
2. Yes, he did.
3. Yes, he did.
4. No, he didn't.
5. Yes, he did.

Inference Questions

1. true
2. true
3. false

Words with More Than One Meaning

1. b
2. b
3. b

Vocabulary Practice

A. 1. route
    2. sea
    3. trip
    4. map
    5. read
    6. born
    7. became
    8. German
    9. later
    10. called
    11. October
    12. queen
    13. discovery

B. B. sea
    A. sailor
    B. singer, money, became
    A. thought
    B. October
    A. stories
    B. ship
    A. land

Word Forms

A. 1. a. Italy
       b. Italian
    2. a. Spanish
       b. Spain
    3. a. Germany
       b. German
    4. a. India
       b. Indian
    5. a. American
       b. America

B. 1. a. sailor
       b. sail
    2. a. explorer
       b. explore
    3. a. discover
       b. discovery
    4. a. writer
       b. write
    5. a. reader
       b. read

Prepositions

1. in
2. to
3. for
4. for
5. on
6. to
7. about
8. on

Numbers

A. 1. three
    2. ten
    3. fourteen

B. 1. 12
    2. 1492

Make A Sentence

1. Christopher Columbus loved the sea.
2. The Spanish queen gave him three ships.
3. The sailors saw land.
4. Columbus didn't discover a new route to India.
5. He discovered a new land.

6. Columbus called the people "Indians."
7. Amerigo Vespucci wrote about this new land.
8. A German mapmaker read Amerigo's stories.
9. He liked them.

Chunking

Christopher Columbus / was born / in Genoa, Italy. / He loved /
    1   2   3   5

the sea. / When he was only fourteen, / he became / a sailor. /
   4   6   5   4

Later, / he became / an explorer. / He wanted to discover /
  8   5   4   5 (and 2)

a new route to India. / The Spanish queen, / Isabella, / gave him
         4   1   7   5

three ships, / sailors, / and money / for his trip. /
      4   7   7   3

Columbus and his sailors / were at sea / for ten weeks. /
           1   5   3

Finally, / on October 12, / 1492, / they saw land. / Columbus
   8   3   7   5

thought / it was India. / He called / the people there "Indians." /
   5   4   5   4

Columbus didn't discover / a new route to India; / he discovered
           5   4   5

a new land. /
     4

Later, / Amerigo Vespucci, / another Italian explorer, / wrote
  8   1   7   2

about / this new land. / A German mapmaker / read Amerigo's
          4   1   5

stories. / He liked them so much that / on the map of Columbus's
                     5   3

India, / he wrote "America"! /
             5

2. Ms. Liberty

Comprehension Questions

A. 1. true
   2. false
   3. false
   4. false
   5. true
   6. false

B. 1. Yes, it is.
   2. No, it isn't.
   3. Yes, it is.

Inference Questions

1. false
2. true
3. true
4. false

Words with More Than One Meaning

1. a
2. b
3. a
4. b

Vocabulary Practice

A. 1. torch
   2. crown
   3. tablet
   4. island
   5. visitor
   6. pedestal
   7. statue
B. 1. symbol
   2. tall
   3. copper
   4. crown
   5. boxes
   6. monument
   7. island
   8. torch
   9. date
   10. hand
   11. size
   12. visitor
   13. lonely
   14. arrive
   15. tablets

Word Forms

A. 1. a. visitor
      b. visit
   2. a. life
      b. live
      c. lively
      d. alive
   3. a. arrival
      b. arrive
   4. a. immigrate
      b. immigrant
      c. Immigration
   5. a. freedom
      b. free
      c. freely
      d. free

B. 1. a. alone   3. a. Gold
    b. Loneliness   b. Golden
    c. lonely   c. gold
   2. a. beautiful   4. a. nation
    b. beauty   b. national

Prepositions

1. on   10. in
2. to   11. to
3. In   12. on
4. In   13. in
5. with   14. On
6. to   15. of
7. from   16. beside
8. in   17. to
9. in   18. of

Numbers

A. 1. ninety-two   B. 1. 4
   2. one   2. 1776
                        3. 1885

Make A Sentence

1. The Statue of Liberty came from France.
2. It holds a torch and a tablet.
3. The date on the tablet is July 4, 1776.
4. The statue is very tall.
5. The Statue of Liberty is a symbol of freedom.
6. It welcomes immigrants and visitors.
7. It is a national monument.
8. The statue's full name is "Liberty Enlightening the World."

Controlled Writing

I live alone on a island, but I'm not lonely. I have visitors all the time. They come to admire my beauty and my size. I am very tall—ninety-two meters. In my right hand, I hold a torch. In my left hand, I hold a tablet with the date July 4, 1776. I wear a copper crown.

I came to America from France in 1885. I arrived in New York in many boxes. It was a big job to put me together. It took one year.

I stand on a pedestal made in America. On the base of the pedestal, it says, "I lift my lamp beside the golden door." I welcome immigrants and visitors to this land.

I am a national monument and a symbol of freedom. I am the Statue of Liberty. My full name is "Liberty Enlightening the World."

Chunking

She lives alone / on an island, / but she isn't lonely. / She has visitors / all the time. / They come to admire / her beauty and her size. / She is very tall— / ninety-two meters. / In her right hand, / she holds / a torch. / In her left hand, / she holds / a tablet with the date July 4, / 1776. / She wears / a copper crown. /

She came / to America / from France / in 1885. / She arrived / in New York / in many boxes. / It was a big job / to put her together. / It took / one year. /

She stands / on a pedestal made in America. / On the base of the pedestal, / it says, / "I lift / my lamp / beside the golden door." / She welcomes / immigrants and visitors / to this land. /

She is / a national monument and a symbol of freedom. / She is / the Statue of Liberty. / Her full name is / "Liberty Enlightening the World." /

3. The Stars and Stripes

Comprehension Questions

A. 1. true
2. true
3. false
4. false
5. true
6. false

B. 1. No, it didn't.
2. Yes, it did.
3. Yes, it did.
4. No, it didn't.

Inference Questions

1. false
2. true
3. true

Words with More Than One Meaning

1. a
2. b
3. a

Vocabulary Practice

1. England
2. flag
3. young
4. represents
5. dressmaker
6. colors
7. design
8. stripes
9. stars
10. square
11. different

Word Forms

1. a. independent
   b. independence
2. a. color
   b. colorful
3. a. different
   b. difference
4. a. representative
   b. represent
5. a. England
   b. English
   c. English

Prepositions

1. in
2. After
3. of
4. on
5. of
6. on
7. for

Numbers

A. 1. thirteen
   2. first
   3. two
   4. fifty
B. 1. 1775
   2. 14
   3. 1777
   4. 1783

Make A Sentence

1. England had thirteen colonies.
2. The colonies became independent.
3. The new country needed a new flag.
4. Betsy Ross made the first U.S. flag.
5. Betsy Ross's flag had stars and stripes.
6. Each star represented one state.
7. The United States has fifty states.
8. The U.S. flag has fifty stars.
9. The Stars and Stripes is the U.S. flag.

Chunking

A long time ago, / England had thirteen colonies / in America. / These colonies / had the same flag as England. / After the Revolutionary War / (1775–1783), / the colonies / became an independent country called the United States of America. / The new country / needed a new flag. /

Betsy Ross, / a Philadelphia dressmaker, / made the first United States flag. / She used / the same colors as the English flag— / red, / white, / and blue— / but her design / was different. / Betsy Ross's flag / had red and white stripes and thirteen white stars on a blue square. / Each star represented / one state. / This became / the official flag of the U.S.A. / on June 14, / 1777. /

The young country grew. / There were / more and more states. / The last two states / were Alaska and Hawaii. / Today, / the United States flag / has fifty white stars— / one for each state. / This flag / has thirteen red and white stripes. / The stripes represent / the thirteen original states. / Americans call their flag / the Stars and Stripes. /

4. Uncle Sam

Comprehension Questions

A. 1. true
   2. true
   3. false
   4. true
   5. false

   6. false

B. 1. No, he didn't.
   2. Yes, it did.
   3. Yes, it did.

Inference Questions

1. true
2. true
3. false

Skimming

1. Sam, Uncle Sam, Samuel Wilson
2. top hat, coat, vest, striped pants
3. 1800s, 1961

Words with More Than One Meaning

1. a
2. b

Vocabulary Practice

A. 1. top hat
   2. hair
   3. whiskers
   4. vest
   5. finger
   6. coat
B. 1. pants
   2. uncle
   3. vest
   4. coat
   5. upstate

6. meat
7. army
8. boxes
9. soldiers
10. cartoon
11. picture
12. popular
13. posters
14. point
15. believe
16. Congress

Word Forms

1. a. businessman
   b. business
2. a. name
   b. name
3. a. friend
   b. friendly
4. a. mean
   b. meaning

5. a. begin
   b. beginning
6. a. government
   b. governor
7. a. official
   b. office
   c. officially

Prepositions

1. in
2. in
3. in
4. to
5. on
6. of
7. to
8. about

9. in
10. During
11. with
12. of
13. for
14. After
15. in
16. from

Numbers

1. 1800s

2. 1961

Make A Sentence

1. Every American has the same uncle.
2. He wears a vest and striped pants.
3. Samuel Wilson was a businessman.

4. He sold meat.
5. Soldiers ate Uncle Sam's meat.
6. The army used a poster with a picture of Uncle Sam.
7. Uncle Sam's picture became popular.
8. Everybody called the U.S. government "Uncle Sam."
9. The name "Uncle Sam" came from Samuel Wilson.

Chunking

Every American / has the same uncle— / Uncle Sam. / He has long white hair and whiskers. / He wears / a top hat, / coat, / vest, / and striped pants. / How did everybody get / the same uncle? /

In the early 1800s, / there was / a businessman / in upstate New York. / His name / was Samuel Wilson. / He was friendly, / and people called him "Uncle Sam." / Uncle Sam / was in the meat business. / He sold meat / to the United States army. / He always wrote / "U.S." / on his boxes of meat. / What did "U.S." mean— / Uncle Sam / or United States? /

American soldiers / ate Uncle Sam's meat. / They began to call / the U.S. government "Uncle Sam." / Soon, / there were cartoons about Uncle Sam / in the newspapers. / His picture / became popular. / During World War I, / there was / a famous poster with a picture of Uncle Sam. / Uncle Sam / pointed his finger and said, / "I WANT YOU FOR U.S. ARMY." /

After this poster, / everybody called / the U.S. government / "Uncle Sam." / Some people / didn't believe / there really was an Uncle Sam Wilson. / But in 1961, / Congress said officially / that the name "Uncle Sam" / came from Samuel Wilson. /

5. 1600 Pennsylvania Avenue, Washington, D.C.

Comprehension Questions

A. 1. true
  2. true
  3. false
  4. false
  5. true
  6. false
  7. true

  8. true
B. 1. Yes, it was.
  2. Yes, it was.
  3. No, it wasn't.
  4. No, it wasn't.
  5. No, it wasn't.

Inference Questions

1. true
2. false

3. false
4. true

Skimming

1. 1792, 1800, 1812, 1745

Words with More Than One Meaning

1. a
2. b
3. a
4. b

Vocabulary Practice

1. white
2. army
3. actress
4. house
5. section

6. War
7. President
8. story
9. front
10. ordinary

Word Forms

1. a. building
   b. build
   c. rebuild
2. a. paint
   b. painting
   c. paint
3. a. architect
   b. architecture

4. a. compete
   b. competition
5. a. win
   b. winner
6. a. designer
   b. design

Prepositions

1. at
2. of
3. with
4. in
5. of
6. of
7. for
8. to
9. from
10. At
11. in
12. of
13. in
14. to

15. in
16. in
17. during
18. of
19. after
20. in
21. of
22. in
23. of
24. in
25. in
26. in
27. at
28. in

Numbers

1. 1600
2. 107
3. $500.
4. 1792
5. 1800
6. 1812
7. 1745

Make A Sentence

1. The White House has 107 rooms.
2. One room is the Oval Office.
3. The building was made of limestone.
4. The architect was James Hoban.
5. Hoban won a competition.
6. He designed the President's house.
7. The British army burned the building.
8. The house at 1600 Pennsylvania Avenue is famous.

Chunking

The white house at 1600 Pennsylvania Avenue / is not / an ordinary house. / The President of the United States / lives there. /

The White House / is a three-story building, / with columns / in the front and back. / It has 107 rooms. / One of them / is the famous Oval Office. /The building / was made of limestone, / a gray stone. / Later, / it was painted white. /

The architect for the President's house / was James Hoban. / Hoban immigrated to the United States / from Ireland. / At that time, / in America, / there was an architecture competition. / Hoban won the competition. / He got $500, / a piece of land in Washington, / D.C., / and the chance to design / the President's house. /

Work began in 1792 / and ended in 1800. / But during the War of 1812, / the British army / burned the building. / The President's house / was destroyed. / Hoban helped rebuild the White House / after the war. /

There is another white house / in a quiet section of Dublin, / Ireland. / It looks very much like / the one in Washington. / People think this house / is a copy of the White House in Washington. / But the fact is / that the house in Dublin / was built / in 1745. /

Maybe the White House at 1600 Pennsylvania Avenue / is not the most original white house in the world, / but it is probably / the most famous. /

6. The First Oil Well in the World

Comprehension Questions

A. 1. true
2. false
3. false
4. true
5. true
6. false
7. false

8. false
9. true

B. 1. Yes, he did.
2. Yes, he did.
3. No, he didn't.
4. No, he didn't.

Inference Questions

1. false
2. true
3. true
4. true

Skimming

1. Titusville, Pennsylvania, New York, Washington, United States

Synonyms

1. business
2. openings
3. popular

4. largest
5. saying

Antonyms

1. new
2. popular
3. importer
4. good
5. end
6. imports

7. largest
8. died
9. poor
10. first
11. successful

Words with More Than One Meaning

1. a
2. a
3. a
4. b

Vocabulary Practice

1. drilled	11. exporter
2. historic	12. saying
3. successful	13. imports
4. Pennsylvania	14. half
5. oil	15. importer
6. medical	16. patent
7. industry	17. lost
8. ground	18. poor
9. modern	19. pension
10. largest	20. billion

Word Forms

1. a. history	7. a. opening
b. historic	b. open
2. a. drill	8. a. new
b. drill	b. news
3. a. oil	9. a. exporter
b. oily	b. export
4. a. successful	10. a. saying
b. success	b. say
5. a. light	11. a. import
b. light	b. importer
c. lighting	12. a. die
6. a. medical	b. death
b. medicine	

Prepositions

1. In	14. of
2. for	15. in
3. in	16. in
4. in	17. to
5. of	18. of
6. for	19. In
7. from	20. in
8. in	21. For
9. of	22. to
10. by	23. on
11. for	24. from
12. for	25. in
13. By	26. after

Numbers

A. 1. first
    2. twenty-one
    3. one billion dollars

B. 1. 1859
    2. 1800s

Make A Sentence

1. Titusville, Pennsylvania is a historic place.
2. Edwin Drake drilled for oil.
3. Drilling for oil was something new.
4. Drake's discovery started the oil industry.
5. Drake's drilling method became very popular.
6. The U.S. imports about half of its oil.
7. Drake never got a patent.
8. He didn't make any money.
9. He lived a poor life.
10. The Pennsylvania government gave him a pension.
11. Drake died a poor man.

Chunking

Titusville, / Pennsylvania, / is not / New York or Washington, / but it / is still a historic place. / In 1859, / a man named Edwin Drake / drilled for oil /in Titusville. / This was the first successful oil well / in the world. /

For hundreds of years, / people used oil / for lighting purposes and medical purposes. / They got this oil / from seepages— / small openings / in the ground. / This oil / came out of the ground / by itself. / But drilling for oil / was something completely new. / Drake's invention / started the oil industry. /

The modern world / needed oil / for everyday life. / Drake's drilling method / became very popular. / By the end of the 1800s, / oil was discovered / in fourteen states. / The United States / became the largest oil exporter / in the world. /

There is a saying / that all good things / come to an end. / Now, / the U.S. imports / about half of its oil. / In fact, / the United States / is the largest oil importer / in the world. /

For Edwin Drake, / all good things / came to an end too. / Drake never got a patent / on his drilling method. / He didn't make any money / from his invention. / He even lost money / in the oil business. / He lived a very poor life. / Finally, / the Pennsylvania government / gave him / a pension. / Drake died a poor man / twenty-one years / after his historic, / billion-dollar invention. /

7. Prohibition

Comprehension Questions

A. 1. Yes, it does.
2. Yes, it does.
3. Yes, it does.
B. 1. No, it didn't.
2. Yes, it did.
3. Yes, they did.
4. No, they didn't.
5. Yes, they did.
C. 1. Gangsters controlled the liquor business during Prohibition.
2. People went to speakeasies to drink during Prohibition.
3. They spoke softly when they ordered drinks during Prohibition.
4. Illegal liquor was called "moonshine" during Prohibition.
5. Prohibition lasted thirteen years in the U.S.

Inference Questions

1. true
2. false
3. true

Skimming

1. liquor stores, bars, restaurants, speakeasies
2. to buy drinks in a speakeasy, to make "moonshine," to transport liquor or "bootlegging"
3. freedom of speech, freedom of religion, freedom of the press, freedom to drink

Synonyms

1. alcohol
2. make
3. transport

Antonyms

1. sell
2. illegal
3. closed
4. big
5. ended

Words with More Than One Meaning

1. a
2. b

Vocabulary Practice

1. Amendment	10. restaurant
2. religion	11. illegal
3. press	12. ordered
4. freedom	13. alcohol
5. drink	14. bottles
6. law	15. Constitution
7. crime	16. Prohibition
8. liquor	17. gangster
9. bar	18. ended

Word Forms

1. a. speak
   b. speech
2. a. religious
   b. religion
3. a. lawyer
   b. law

   c. illegal
   d. legal
4. a. drink
   b. drink
   c. drinking

Prepositions

1. of	14. to
2. In	15. to
3. to	16. During
4. to	17. of
5. With	18. in
6. to	19. in
7. in	20. from
8. to	21. to
9. at	22. In
10. to	23. to
11. in	24. to
12. of	25. about
13. to	

Numbers

A. 1. eighteenth
   2. twenty-first

B. 1. 1933
   2. 1920

Make A Sentence

1. Americans didn't have the freedom to drink during Prohibition.
2. Bars didn't sell alcohol.
3. People drank liquor in speakeasies.
4. People carried bottles in the leg of their boot.
5. Gangsters controlled the illegal liquor business.
6. "Bootlegging" got a new meaning.
7. The Twenty-first Amendment canceled the Eighteenth Amendment.
8. Americans have the freedom to drink today.

Chunking

The American Constitution / guarantees freedom of speech, / religion, / and the press. / In 1920, / a new law / (the Eighteenth Amendment), / was added / to the Constitution. / This law said that Americans / did not have the freedom to drink. /

With a new law, / there are often new crimes. / Liquor stores, / bars, / and restaurants didn't sell alcohol. / But some people wanted to drink. / They drank in secret, / illegal places. / When they ordered drinks, / they spoke softly. / That's why such a place was called a "speakeasy." /

It was illegal to make alcohol. / Liquor companies were closed. / But people made alcohol secretly, / at night. / This illegal alcohol was called "moonshine." /

It was also illegal to sell or carry alcohol. / When people sold alcohol, / they carried the bottles in the leg of their boot. / This crime was called "bootlegging." /

The time when it was illegal to drink, / to make, / or to sell alcohol was called Prohibition. / During Prohibition, / gangsters controlled the liquor business. / They organized the production of "moonshine" / and sold it in their "speakeasies." / It was a big business. / "Bootlegging" got a new meaning. / Gangsters transported liquor in cars, / trucks, / and ships. /

Prohibition didn't stop people from drinking. / But it added new crimes to American life. / In 1933, / Prohibition ended. / A new law was added to the Constitution / (the Twenty-first Amendment). / It canceled the Eighteenth Amendment. / Now, / in America, / people have the "freedom" to drink. / What do you think about this freedom? /

8. The American Folk Hero

Comprehension Questions

A. 1. Yes, he is.
   2. No, he isn't.

3. Yes, he is.
4. Yes, he is.
B. 1. Yes, they did.
2. No, they didn't.
3. No, they didn't.
4. Yes, they did.
5. Yes, they did.
C. 1. Buffalo Bill killed 4,280 buffaloes.
2. The folk heroes in other countries are the prince, the soldier, or the sailor.
3. The cowboy wears a cowboy hat, cowboy boots, and a pair of jeans.
4. Movies made the cowboy famous all over the world.
5. Cowboys moved cattle north and west in the early 1800s.

Inference Questions

1. true
2. true
3. false

Skimming

1. prince, soldier, sailor, cowboy
2. horse, cattle, buffalo
3. America, Canada

Pronouns

1. a
2. b
3. b

Synonyms

1. fairy tales
2. rodeos
3. famous

Antonyms

1. dirty
2. dangerous
3. friend

Words with More Than One Meaning

1. b   3. a
2. a

Vocabulary Practice

1. gun   10. lasso
2. cowboy   11. Bill
3. whiskey   12. rodeo
4. bandits   13. boots
5. dangerous   14. dirty
6. horse   15. branding iron
7. fairy tale   16. Pacific
8. Canada   17. prince
9. railroad

Word Forms

1. a. work   4. a. live
   b. worker   b. life
2. a. hand   5. a. ride
   b. handle   b. rider
3. a. rob   6. a. killer
   b. robber   b. kill

Prepositions

1. In   8. In
2. In   9. to
3. In   10. to
4. On   11. of
5. On   12. with
6. from   13. to
7. from   14. on

Numbers

1. 1800s   2. 4,280

Make A Sentence

1. The cowboy is a romantic figure.
2. His life is an adventure.
3. He chases trains.

4. The cowboy uses a lasso and a gun.
5. The American folk hero came from real life.
6. Real cowboys helped win the West.
7. Buffalo Bill was a famous cowboy.
8. He killed 4,280 buffaloes.
9. Buffalo Bill organized rodeos.

Chunking

In some countries, / the folk hero is the prince. / In other countries, / it is the soldier or the sailor. / In America, / the folk hero is the cowboy. / He wears a cowboy hat, / cowboy boots, / and a pair of jeans. /

On the one hand, / the cowboy is a romantic figure. / His life is an adventure. / He chases trains and robs banks. / He drinks whiskey, / fights bandits, / and helps women. /

On the other hand, / the cowboy is a hard worker. / His job is dirty and dangerous. / He rides a horse and rounds up cattle. / He uses a lasso, / a branding iron, / and a gun. / He handles each one masterfully. /

The American folk hero didn't come from fairy tales. / He came from real life. / In the early 1800s, / real cowboys moved cattle north to Canada and west to the Pacific Ocean. / These cowboys helped win the West. /

Buffalo Bill was one of the most famous cowboys. / He was a great rider, / buffalo hunter, / Indian fighter, / and Indian friend. / He got the name "Buffalo Bill" because he killed 4,280 buffaloes. / What did he do with all that buffalo meat? / He distributed it to the people working on the railroad. /

Buffalo bill was also a showman. / He organized cowboy shows, / or rodeos. / He called his group "The Wild West." / There were buffalo hunts, / shooting contests, / and cowboy and Indian fights. /

Rodeos made the cowboy popular all over America. / Movies made this folk hero famous all over the world. /

9. Fall Back, Spring Ahead

Comprehension Questions

A. 1. Yes, they are.
   2. No, they aren't.
   3. Yes, they were.
   4. Yes, it does.
   5. No, they don't.
B. 1. Clocks are moved ahead in America on the last Sunday in April.
   2. Clocks are moved back in America on the last Sunday in October.

3. Benjamin Franklin suggested Daylight Saving Time in 1784.
4. Daylight Saving Time became a law in 1966.
5. We call the time from the last Sunday in October to the last Sunday in April Standard Time.
6. We call the time from the last Sunday in April to the last Sunday in October Daylight Saving Time.
7. Clocks were changed in America during World War I and II to save electricity.
8. Benjamin Franklin suggested Daylight Saving Time in an essay.

Inference Questions

1. true
2. false
3. true

Skimming

1. April, October
2. 1784, 1966
3. spring, summer, fall

Pronouns

1. b
2. a
3. b

Synonyms

1. back
2. ended
3. suggested
4. usually

Antonyms

1. last
2. remember
3. joking
4. necessary
5. save
6. earlier
7. less

Words with More Than One Meaning

1. b
2. a
3. a

Vocabulary Practice

1. clock
2. law
3. simple
4. started
5. fall
6. energy
7. experiment
8. essay
9. suggested
10. story
11. Spring
12. electricity

Word Forms

1. a. change
   b. change
2. a. year
   b. yearly
3. a. memory
   b. remember
4. a. need
   b. necessity
   c. necessary

Prepositions

1. in
2. On
3. On
4. to
5. to
6. behind
7. in
8. in
9. during
10. to
11. to
12. In
13. To
14. of
15. at
16. at
17. at
18. in
19. at
20. of
21. During
22. until
23. to
24. To

Numbers

1. 1784
2. 1966

Make A Sentence

1. Many people can't remember to change their clocks.
2. Benjamin Franklin suggested Daylight Saving Time.
3. The country needed energy.
4. Changing the clocks was an experiment.
5. People had an extra hour of daylight.
6. They used less electricity.
7. Daylight Saving Time became a law.
8. Americans say "Fall back, spring ahead."

Sentence Scramble

1. Americans usually like the spring.
2. He can't remember when the summer starts.
3. She wrote an essay about time.
4. Last Sunday, he told us a story about the war.

Chunking

Two times a year, / clocks are changed in America. / It's a law. / On the last Sunday in April, / clocks are moved ahead one hour. / This is called Daylight Saving Time. / On the last Sunday in October, / clocks are moved back one hour to Standard Time. / It's very simple, / but many people can't remember to change their clocks. / Maybe that's because they don't know the story behind it. /

It all started back in 1784. / Benjamin Franklin, / an American writer, / diplomat, / and inventor, / suggested Daylight Saving Time in an essay. / People thought he was joking. /

Many years later, / during World War I and World War II, / people realized that Benjamin Franklin was right. / The country needed energy. / It was necessary to save electricity, / but how? / One way was to change the time. / In the spring and summer, / the sun rises earlier. / To take advantage of this early sunlight, / clocks were moved ahead one hour. / So now, / people who usually woke up at 8:00 really woke up at 7:00. / If they normally turned on the lights at 5:00 in the evening, / now they turned on the lights at 6:00. / They had an extra hour of daylight, / so they used less electricity. /

During the wars, / changing the clocks was just an experiment. / Daylight Saving Time didn't become a law until 1966. / But this didn't make it any easier to remember. / People still asked each other, / "When do you change the time, / and which way?" / To make it a little easier, / Americans just say, / "Fall back, spring ahead." /

10. **This Land Is Your Land**

Comprehension Questions

A. 1. Yes, he did.
2. Yes, he did.
3. No, he didn't.
4. Yes, he did.
5. Yes, he did.
6. No, he didn't.
7. No, he didn't.
8. No, he didn't.

B. 1. When Woody Guthrie was a boy he lived in a small town in Oklahoma.
   2. His sister died in an accident.
   3. He traveled across the country by train.
   4. He carried a guitar and a harmonica when he traveled.
   5. He wrote more than one thousand songs.
   6. His first album came out in 1940.
   7. Woody Guthrie wanted to be free.

Inference Questions

1. true
2. true

3. false
4. true

Skimming

1. selling newspapers, shining shoes, picking grapes, drilling for oil, painting signs, washing dishes, singing songs, writing songs
2. hobo songs, work songs, peace songs, war songs
3. at parties, at rodeos, in bars, at home

Pronouns

1. a
2. b
3. b

Synonyms

1. small
2. easy
3. cheap

4. optimistic
5. record

Antonyms

1. sold
2. back
3. peace
4. poor

5. happy
6. good
7. first

Words with More Than One Meaning

1. b
2. a
3. a

Vocabulary Practice

1. town
2. mental
3. burned
4. accident
5. shined
6. picked
7. dishes
8. train
9. baggage
10. guitar
11. minstrels
12. cheap
13. back
14. war
15. peace
16. classics
17. poor
18. optimistic
19. folk
20. radio
21. record
22. album
23. businessman
24. fame
25. free

Word Forms

1. a. singer
   b. song
   c. sing
2. a. die
   b. death
3. a. shiny
   b. shine
4. a. paint
   b. paint
   c. painter
5. a. seat
   b. sit
6. a. peaceful
   b. peace
7. a. music
   b. musician
8. a. classical
   b. classics
9. a. record
   b. record
   c. record

Prepositions

1. in
2. in
3. in
4. in
5. to
6. At
7. on
8. for
9. across
10. by
11. at
12. at
13. in
14. at
15. of
16. with
17. of
18. about
19. on
20. In
21. to
22. to
23. on
24. of
25. to

Numbers

A. 1. one thousand   B. 1. 1912
   2. fifteen   2. 1940
   3. twentieth

Make A Sentence

1. Woody Guthrie was a singer and a songwriter.
2. He shined shoes.
3. He sold newspapers.
4. "Home" was a friend's apartment.
5. The little guy with the guitar sang hobo songs and work songs.
6. He couldn't read music.
7. Many of his songs became American classics.
8. They were optimistic songs.
9. A record company recorded his songs.
10. Woodie Guthrie didn't want money or fame.
11. He wanted to be free.

Chunking

Woody Guthrie was a singer and a songwriter. / He was born in 1912 / in a small town in Oklahoma. / Life wasn't easy when he was a boy. / His house burned down. / His sister died in an accident. / His mother went to a mental institution. / At fifteen, / Woody didn't have a family anymore. /

He was on his own. / He sold newspapers. / He shined shoes. / He picked grapes and drilled for oil. / He painted signs and washed dishes. / He traveled across the country by train. / His baggage was a guitar and a harmonica. / He was a twentieth-century traveling minstrel. / He sang at parties, / at rodeos, / in bars, / and at home. / "Home" was usually a friend's apartment, / a cheap hotel, / or the back seat of a car. /

The little guy with the guitar / sang hobo songs and work songs: /

> *You get a hammer and I'll get a nail, /*
> *You catch a bird and I'll catch a snail, /*
> *You bring a board and I'll bring a saw, /*
> *And we'll build a house for the baby-o. / ©*

He sang peace songs and war songs, too: /

> *I didn't boil myself no coffee, /*
> *I didn't boil no tea, /*
> *I made a run for that recruitin' office /*
> *Uncle Sam, make room for me! / ©*

Woody Guthrie couldn't read music, / but he wrote more than one thousand songs. / Many of them became American classics. / They were about working people, / poor people, / hungry people. / But they were happy songs, / optimistic songs. / "I hate a song that makes you think that you're not any good," / Woody said. /

Woody Guthrie, / the folk singer, / was becoming popular. / His music was on the radio. / A record company recorded his songs. / In 1940, / his first album came out. / Businessmen wanted to control him. / They told him what to do. / But Woody didn't listen, / and, / once again, / he was on the road. /

Woody Guthrie didn't want money. / He didn't want fame. / He was a true son of his country. / He wanted to be free. /

> *This land is your land, / this land is my land /*
> *From California / to the New York island. /*
> *From the Redwood Forest / to the Gulf Stream waters /*
> *This land was made for you and me. / ©*

Current and Forthcoming Titles on HBJ's ESL List

Reading

Greg Costa   *American Short Stories*

Mira B. Felder and Anna Bryks Bromberg   *Light and Lively*

Len Fox   *Perspectives*

James M. Hendrickson and Angela Labarca   *The Spice of Life*

Lucette Rollet Kenan
   A Changing Scene
   Fact and Fancy
   Modern American Profiles

Pamela McPartland   *Americana*

Paul Pimsleur, Donald Berger, and Beverly Pimsleur
   Encounters, Second Edition

Grammar

Mary Jane Cook
   Trouble Spots of English Grammar, Volumes 1 and 2

J. N. Hook   *Two-Word Verbs in English*

William E. Rutherford
   Modern English, Second Edition, Volumes 1 and 2

Writing

Barbara Auerbach and Beth Snyder   *Paragraph Patterns*

Len Fox   *Passages*

Conversation

Myrna Knepler   *Let's Talk About It*